Lecture Notes in Computer Science

Edited by G. Goos and J. Hartmanis

302

Daniel M. Yellin

Attribute Grammar Inversion
and
Source-to-source Translation

Springer-Verlag

Berlin Heidelberg New York London Paris Tokyo

Author

Daniel M. Yellin
IBM T.J. Watson Research Center
P.O. Box 704, Yorktown Heights, NY 10598, USA

CR Subject Classification (1987): D.2.7, D.3.1, D.3.4

ISBN 3-540-19072-4 Springer-Verlag Berlin Heidelberg New York
ISBN 0-387-19072-4 Springer-Verlag New York Berlin Heidelberg

© Springer-Verlag Berlin Heidelberg 1988
Printed in Germany

Printing and binding: Druckhaus Beltz, Hemsbach/Bergstr.
2145/3140-543210

Preface

The sage Yiztchak said: If a man tells you:
"I have struggled but have not found", do not believe him.
"I have not struggled but have found", do not believe him.
"I have struggled and have found", believe him.
Babylonian Talmud, Tractate Megilla, 6b

This book describes a new technique for source-to-source translation. Source-to-source translation can be applied to a wide variety of notations: for example, translation of programs from one programming language to another, or translation of documents from one markup language to another.

The technique is based upon attribute grammar technology. Given an attribute grammar describing the translation from language A to B, we show how to automatically derive an inverse attribute grammar, which translates language B to A.

In Part I, we review how attribute grammars are used to define translations between languages. We then present the inversion algorithm, and analyze properties of the translators produced by inversion. In Part II, we show how to apply the principles of Part I to the construction of practical source-to-source translators. We discuss how to factor the translation among a set of languages $L_1, L_2, \ldots, L_n$ into translations between each L_i and a canonical "least common divisor" of the set of languages. A translator between any two source languages is then obtained by inversion and composition of translators. Part II concludes with an illustration of how this methodology is applied to construct Pascal-to-C and C-to-Pascal translators.

This book is based upon my dissertation, completed at Columbia University in the city of New York. First and foremost, I would like to thank my advisor, Rodney Farrow. Many of the ideas of my thesis grew out of our conversations, and many improvements were based upon his insights. More than just facts, he taught me the methodology of computer science research.

I would also like to thank Mike Foster and Ravi Sethi for providing additional perspectives of my work, and many valuable suggestions. Kathy McKeown, along with other members of my committee, carefully reviewed several versions of my thesis, and greatly improved its presentation. I am especially grateful to Eva Mueckstein for encouraging my research during my summers at IBM Yorktown, and to Peter Sweeney for his assistance in implementing portions of the INVERT system.

Finally, I am indebted to my parents and to my wife Rina for their constant love, affection, and support. This book is dedicated to the memory of my mother. Her legacy of devotion, unselfishness, and a striving for perfection, will serve as my everlasting inspiration.

Yorktown Heights, February 1988   Daniel M. Yellin

Table of Contents

List of Figures

Chapter 1

Introduction

Since the development of the electronic computer, much research has been devoted to issues concerning the translation of natural and formal languages. Indeed, it can be argued that the widespread use of computers today is due, in a large part, to the success of this research. Instead of requiring users to program in machine language, a tedious and error-prone process, translation techniques allow them to use a high level abstract language, well-suited to the problem domain. Programs written in these languages are then automatically converted to machine readable instructions.

Translators are taking on more and more tasks in the realm of software applications. Where once confined to the roles of assemblers and compilers, today translators are commonly used as command processors, as tools to draw pictures, and as VLSI "compilers", programs that produce low level layouts of electronic circuits from abstract descriptions. By formulating a software task in terms of a translation problem, the programmer is able to bring to the task both a rich and elegant theory as well as efficient and effective development tools. Translation technology is applicable to a wide range of problems.

In the early days of computer science, the focus of translation research centered on the role of syntax. A theory of parsing evolved (see, for instance, [8]). After developing a formalism for describing the structure of sentences of a language, researchers devised algorithms to determine whether or not a sentence was valid for a given language. This in turn lead to programs called *parser generators*. These programs take a declarative description of the syntax of a language and automatically produce an efficient program to recognize all the valid sentences of that language. With the advent of tools to aid in the building of translators, translation technology took a giant step forward.

More recently, research has centered on the semantics of languages. After discovering several ways of describing the meaning and translation of languages in a precise manner, researchers began to analyze the characteristics of these formalisms. This theory once again led to the creation of tools to aid in the translation process. The result has been programs called *compiler compilers*. These tools take a declarative description of a translation and produce an efficient program that translates according to the specification. Since the creation of a translator by hand can involve an immense amount of software, these tools promise to greatly enhance translation technology. Not only do they automate much software development, they also guarantee that the translator is faithful to its specification, thereby increasing reliability.

The research discussed in this thesis extends existing translation theory and introduces a new translation tool. The way in which it extends existing theory is in its formulation of *bi-directional* translators. A bi-directional translator is one that translates between two languages **in either direction**. This is in contrast to a **uni-directional** translator which only translates from a source language to a target language, but not vice versa. A bi-directional translator must be symmetric; that is, if going in one direction the string w is translated to the string x, then when going in the reverse direction the string x must be translated to w. This property is referred to as *consistency*. Using current technology, a bi-directional translator can only be made by first specifying the language-to-language mapping in one direction and then specifying the language-to-language mapping in the reverse direction. Not only does the need for two distinct specifications double the labor involved in creating a bi-directional translator, it also makes it difficult to insure that consistency is maintained. Indeed, since these specifications are often long and complex, it is very likely that they will not be consistent.

The research described in this thesis shows that with relatively little extra effort, a uni-directional translation specification can be used to specify a bi-directional translator instead of a uni-directional one. This is accomplished by taking the uni-directional translation specification, an attribute grammar, and inverting it to produce the inverse specification. In order for this to be done <u>automatically</u>, many technical obstacles need to be overcome. Much of the work of this thesis analyzes and solves these technical difficulties. Using *attribute grammar inversion*, it is possible to construct a *two-way compiler compiler*. Unlike the compiler compilers in existence today which accept an attribute grammar and produce a uni-directional translator, a two-way compiler compiler takes an attribute grammar as input and produces a <u>bi-directional</u> translator as output.

A major incentive for developing bi-directional translators is to aid in the quest for software reusability. In particular, using the theory and tools of attribute grammar inversion this thesis will present a methodology for constructing source-to-source translators. This methodology will help to automate the process of moving software from one language environment to another. With the tremendous proliferation of programming languages, dialects, and environments, source-to-source translators will play an important role in prolonging the life and usefulness of software. By automating the routine task of rewriting software, it has the potential to drastically increase program development productivity. To demonstrate the feasibility of this approach to source-to-source translation, it has been used to build translators between the Pascal and C programming languages. These translators will also be discussed in this thesis.

The rest of this chapter will introduce the subject matter of this thesis in more depth. The next section will briefly review grammar based translation methodologies. This is intended to put the ideas of this thesis in the context of traditional compiler theory (ala [4]). It will also introduce the central technical problem this thesis will solve: how to automatically invert translation specifications (attribute grammars) to obtain the inverse specifications. This inversion technique will play the central role in the construction of bi-directional translators. In section 1.2 several applications of bi-directional translators will be given. In particular, it will be shown how they can be used to create source-to-source translators. Section 1.3 will discuss previous related work and the last section of the chapter will provide an overview to the rest of the thesis.

1.1. Grammar based translation methodologies

Over the last several years, much research has been conducted in the use of specifications for translations. Specifying a translation in a formal manner has many benefits. First of all, assuming that the target language is well understood, the formal translation description can serve as an unambiguous statement as to the meaning of the source language. To resolve any conflict in the interpretation of a source language sentence, the specification is consulted and the translation of the sentence is unequivocally determined.

Secondly, some specification methods are non-procedural in nature and allow for the automatic generation of software. These specification methods consist of a declarative set of rules which, when applied to a source language sentence, unambiguously determines its translation. The actual implementation of the rules is not specified. As a matter of fact, such a specification of a translation may have many different implementations. This use of non-procedurality is not new to translator-writing systems. For many years, the syntax of programming languages has been specified declaratively by way of context-free grammars. These grammars describe the syntax of languages independent of any parsing algorithm. Although a context-free grammar has many different implementations, i.e., an LL parser, an LR parser, a recursive descent parser, etc., the language they recognize is the same. Formal non-procedural specifications of translations extend this use of non-procedurality to include not only the syntax of languages but the semantics as well.

By specifying the translation in a non-procedural manner, the designer is freed from worrying about implementation details and can concentrate on the abstract and essential features of the translation. The implementation can be constructed automatically after the specification is complete by feeding the specification into a compiler compiler [42, 17, 24, 45, 18], as illustrated in figure 1-1. A compiler compiler takes a description of a language-to-language mapping as input and emits a procedural translator as output. The generated translator is guaranteed to translate strings according to the input specification.

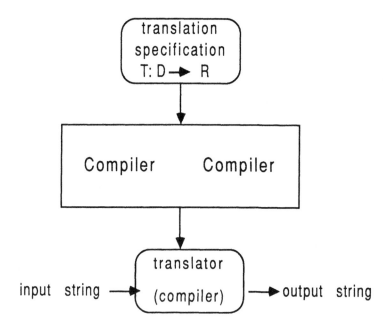

Figure 1-1: A compiler compiler

Several methods of formally specifying translations have been developed. This thesis concentrates on *grammar based translation methodologies*[1]. These methodologies first build a parse tree for the input sentence, similar to the grammar school exercise of diagraming a sentence. After this tree is built, a set of semantic actions are performed on it in order to arrive at the translation. The nature of these actions depends upon the particular translation methodology.

A *syntax-directed translation scheme*, first introduced by Irons [29], arrives at the translation by actually manipulating the parse tree. Branches of the tree are reordered, input symbols deleted, and output symbols added. The result is a parse tree for the output sentence (the translation). A syntax-directed translation scheme is a simple form for expressing a mapping between languages and exhibits a clear relationship between

---

[1] A more meaningful name would be *syntax-directed translation methodologies*. However, in order to avoid confusion between the general class of translations being investigated and the particular translation methodology called syntax-directed translation schema (described below), the less insightful name of grammar based translation methodologies is used.

input sentences and output sentences. Unfortunately, the types of translations that can be performed by these schema are limited. For example, since the output language of a syntax-directed translation scheme is always context-free, no context sensitivities can be reflected in the translation process [5].

Attribute grammars, first introduced by Knuth [43], arrive at the translation not by manipulating the tree but by decorating it with attribute fields and evaluating these fields. One attribute field can be used to define another, but only if the two attributes are adjacent in the tree. The translation is specified to reside in a distinguished attribute of the root. Although attribute grammars restrict the way information can flow through the tree, since any computable function can be used to define an attribute field, attribute grammars are equivalent in power to Turing machines; they can perform any computable translation. One difficulty with attribute grammars, however, is that since the functions describing attribute fields have no predefined structure, it is often difficult to perform useful transformations on them.

The central question this thesis addresses is as follows: Given an attribute grammar specifying the translation T over the finite alphabets $\Sigma \times \Delta$, is there an algorithm to produce the inverse attribute grammar specifying the translation T^{-1} with the property that (w,x) is in T if and only if (x,w) is in T^{-1}?

The following chapters show how this question can be answered in the affirmative. To do so a new grammar based translation methodology will be introduced, *Restricted Inverse Form Grammars (RIFs)*, a cross between syntax-directed translation schema and attribute grammars. Although their basic translation operations permute the parse tree, just like syntax-directed translation schema, they make extensive use of attribute fields to determine how this permutation is to be carried out. This allows these grammars to perform context sensitive translations, making them a practical tool for real compiler-writing systems. Yet, because they are more restricted than attribute grammars they can be analyzed and manipulated more readily, and therefore inverted.

Formally, a RIF can be defined as a restricted attribute grammar. Each nonterminal of a RIF can have an arbitrary number of attributes and each attribute can be defined by an arbitrary function. RIFs differ from attribute grammars in that, additionally, each nonterminal has a distinguished attribute representing the translation of the subtree beneath it. This distinguished attribute must be defined by a special form, essentially allowing it to concatenate and permute its childrens' distinguished attributes, and to add constant tokens of the output alphabet. It can use other nondistinguished attributes only to determine exactly how this permutation is to be performed. Surprisingly, it turns out that RIFs are equivalent in power to attribute grammars; in chapter 2 it is shown that any attribute grammar can be converted to a RIF performing the same translation.

In chapter 3 an algorithm is presented which, given any RIF specifying the translation T over $\Sigma \times \Delta$, will produce the inverse RIF specifying the translation T^{-1} over $\Delta \times \Sigma$. This result, coupled with the procedure converting arbitrary attribute grammars to RIFs provides a method for inverting any attribute grammar. Unfortunately, a strict application of this method will produce an inverse attribute grammar which is terribly ambiguous and inefficient, even if the original attribute grammar was unambiguous and efficient[2]. For this reason much of this thesis explores properties of RIFs and properties of the inversion algorithm. Special consideration is given to finding restrictions and/or extensions to RIFs which give rise to efficient inverses. Chapters 4 and 5 will examine various generalizations of RIFs that accomplish this goal.

The inversion of RIFs is possible because each rule of a RIF expresses a duality between its context free portion and its semantic portion. The inversion algorithm exploits this duality by switching the roles of syntax and semantics. Given any RIF, the inverse attribute grammar produced by the inversion algorithm is also a RIF. Hence RIFs are closed under inversion.

---

[2] By saying that an attribute grammar is inefficient, we mean that it is time consuming, from an algorithmic standpoint, to determine the translation of an input string. This is due to the ambiguity of the grammar. This is explained in more detail in the beginning of chapter 4. See also sections 2.1.1.2, 3.3, 5.3, and 7.1

1.2. Applications of bi-directional translators

The preceding section described how specifications of translations (attribute grammars) can be used to automatically generate translators by feeding the specification into a compiler compiler (figure 1-1). Using restricted attribute grammars (RIFs) to specify translations, we can automatically generate bi-directional translators. This is done by feeding the RIF into a two-way compiler compiler, as illustrated in figure 1-2. The emitted bi-directional translator is capable of translating strings from the domain D into strings of the range R or vice versa.

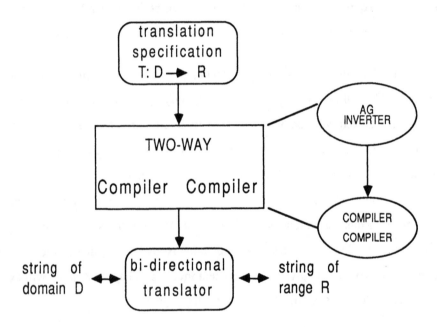

Figure 1-2: A two-way compiler compiler

Bi-directional translators are useful for a variety of tasks. They allow for two-way communication between various systems speaking different dialects or between a user and the computer. For example, a bi-directional translator could be used as a natural language interface between a data base user and the data base query system, as illustrated in figure 1-3. The user could pose his queries in restricted natural language phrases and the translator would translate them into a sentence of the data base query language. Conversely, a data base query could be paraphrased in natural language by the inverse translator. Such a bi-directional translator was actually constructed from a single RIF specification [67].

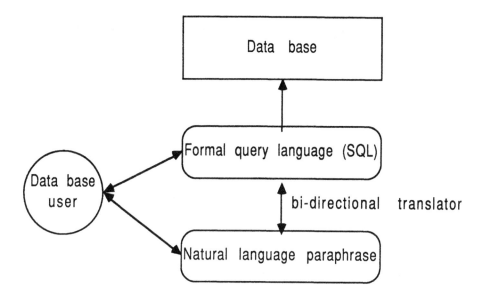

Figure 1-3: A bi-directional translator for data base queries

Of course, a bi-directional translator between the two languages L_1 and L_2 could be constructed from two separate specifications, $T_1: L_1 \rightarrow L_2$ and $T_2: L_2 \rightarrow L_1$. Indeed, if the desired translators are not consistent, i.e., (w,x) is in T_1 but (x,w) is not in T_2, then this is the only option. However, if the translators are to be consistent then RIFs are an ideal specification tool. Not only do they cut the labor in half by requiring only a single specification, they guarantee consistency. If the two specifications were written manually and independently of one another it is unlikely that this property would be preserved. Furthermore, if at some later date one of the RIF-generated translators is updated, the inverse translator can be automatically produced from the updated version, thereby maintaining consistency.

For many problem domains, consistency is an essential requirement. Consider, for instance, a system used to manipulate multiple views of an object. One might like to represent a program as structured text or as a flow diagram. Similarly, one might employ two different VLSI languages to represent VLSI layouts. A bi-directional translator generated from a RIF could be used in this context to translate between these different representations. In this case consistency is an essential feature in order to guarantee that objects converted from one representation to the other and then back again retain their identity.

A major incentive for studying bi-directional translators is in order to build source-to-source translators. The way this is done is illustrated in the diagram of figure 1-4. In this example we would like to translate between the four programming languages, A, B, C, and D. In order to do so, we first write four <u>invertible</u> AGs, T_A, T_B, T_C, and T_D, specifying the translation of each language into a canonical form. We then automatically invert these specifications, obtaining the inverse AGs T_A^{-1}, T_B^{-1}, T_C^{-1}, and T_D^{-1}, specifying the translation from the canonical form back to each programming language . By composing the translators obtained by this method one is able to produce a translator between any pair of languages. For example, the translator from language A to language D can be obtained by composing the specifications T_D^{-1} and T_A. Similarly, its inverse, the translator from language D to language A, is obtained by forming the composition $T_A^{-1} \circ T_D$.

For this method to succeed, we must have a canonical form in which all source language programs can be expressed. We must also be able to write invertible AGs describing the translation from the source languages to the canonical form. In the latter part of this thesis these issues will be examined in depth. It will also describe how the method outlined above was applied to build a bi-directional translator between the Pascal and C programming languages. This was done by formulating a canonical representation, called ABSIM, in which most Pascal and C constructs can be expressed and then writing invertible AGs from the source languages into ABSIM. The INVERT program[3] was subsequently used to automatically generate the inverse AGs. All four

---

[3] INVERT takes an AG in appropriately restricted form and produces another AG that describes the inverse translation.

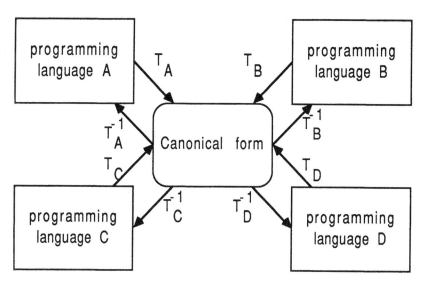

Figure 1-4: Source-to-source translators

AGs (two originals and two generated by INVERT) were then run through the Linguist [19] AG-based translator-writing-system to produce four translators: Pascal-to-ABSIM, ABSIM-to-Pascal, C-to-ABSIM, and ABSIM-to-C. The composition of appropriate pairs of these are the Pascal-to-C and C-to-Pascal translators.

The scheme for source-to-source translation depicted above is not limited specifically to programming languages. The method will work just as well if the "languages" are electronic representations of formatted text [49] or representations of VLSI circuits. The only essential requirements are that (i) there exists a canonical form into which all "languages" can be translated and that (ii) one can write these translations as invertible attribute grammars.

1.3. Related work

This thesis deals with (i) inverting translation specifications, (ii) an analysis of different grammar based translation methodologies (in the context of inversion), and (iii) source-to-source translators. The inversion of translation specifications can be seen as a special case of inverting general purpose programs, of which there has been some discussion in the literature [26, 55, 44]. Because this thesis is working with a restricted, better defined, and more structured problem, the goals, techniques, and results of the thesis are quite different from these works. When we focus on invertibility as it relates to translation specifications, there is far less reported in the literature. In fact, I am only aware of three pieces of work along these lines.

The first work, Reiss' thesis [52], is very similar to my own research in spirit. His goal, to invert translation specifications to assist in automatic programming, is very similar to the goal of inverting attribute grammars to build source-to-source translators. Furthermore, he also uses grammar based translation methodologies as the starting point for his research. Nonetheless, a more detailed look at our two works will reveal important differences. First of all, Reiss considers a range of specifications, the most powerful being generalized syntax-directed translation schemata (see [7]). These grammar based translation methodologies are much weaker than attribute grammars, which are capable of performing any translation. The reason why Reiss did not consider more complex grammar based translation methodologies is because of his complexity results. He found that given a more complex grammar based translation methodology, it is not always possible to build an inverse translator that will operate in polynomial time. It is true that the translation methodology adopted by this thesis, attribute grammars, can, in the worst case, produce very inefficient translators; appendix A proves that the version of attribute grammars used in this thesis can even express uncomputable translations. But the fact that attribute grammars can express such complex translations is not a reason for not using them. Although inverting an arbitrary attribute grammar can result in an impractical translator, the inversion of a well structured attribute grammar will result in a very efficient evaluator. Part of the work in this thesis is aimed at showing how efficiency can be retained even when specifying very complex translations. If we adopt a severely restricted methodology instead of attribute grammars, however, then we are ruling out the inversion of many important sorts of translations[4]. Another reason, perhaps, why Reiss limited his discussion to simpler grammar based translation methodologies is because attribute grammars were not as popular then as they are now. He did not have the wide body of theoretical results and practical experience concerning attribute grammars to draw from that is present today. In suggesting future topics for research, Reiss suggests the use of attribute grammars to express invertible translations. Hence, this work can be seen as a continuation of his. Section 4.2 will compare some technical details of this thesis to Reiss' work.

Another importance difference between our two studies is that the theory developed in this thesis has been applied to build a complete software system, INVERT, implementing attribute grammar inversion. Furthermore, this system has been used to construct translators between the Pascal and C programming languages. Not only has this experience helped adapt the theory of attribute grammar inversion for real world applications, it also provides concrete evidence to the feasibility of the approach. By demonstrating how attribute grammar inversion can be used to build source-to-source translators, it has the potential for becoming a widely used development tool. For example, it has recently been suggested [49] that bi-directional translators formed from AG inversion be used in a system to support the exchange of electronic manuscripts.

The second work concerning bi-directional translators that I am aware of also involves the creation of a translation tool. In [40], a system is discussed which uses the same grammar for both parsing sentences of English into semantic networks and for generating English descriptions from semantic networks. This work focuses more on the natural language issues involved than developing a theory of inversion, and it is hard to compare it to my own research.

---

[4] An analogy can be made to the use of looping constructs in programming languages. These constructs can cause one to write programs that loop infinitely. But this doesn't mean that loops should be discarded from programming languages. Indeed, most programs would be impossible to write without some loop construct. Similarly, if inversion is to be a useful technique, we must be able to invert a translation methodology which offers the writer the possibility of expressing complex translations, even if it also gives him the possibility of writing very inefficient ones. Using weak grammar based translation methodologies would make the system overly restrictive for writing any interesting translations. As described later in this thesis, I even found RIFs difficult to use because of their restrictiveness, and was therefore forced to generalize them.

A third suggestion on inverting translations appears in the works of a few Prolog researchers [9, 15]. They suggest that phrasing translations in a logic programming paradigm (specifically, in Prolog), will gain the added benefit of invertibilty. This is due to the "reversible" nature of Prolog functions. We believe that although there is some merit in this approach, AG inversion is a more promising technology to pursue for four reasons: (1) not all translations can be easily expressed by Prolog programs, (2) AGs are much more efficient than Prolog programs in expressing translations, (3) although Prolog is invertible in theory, it is not so in practice, and (4) since current translation technology is largely dominated by syntax-directed AG-like methodologies, inverting translations written in this manner is important in its own right. In the discussion that follows, which elaborates on these claims, we use attribute grammar terminology in discussing Prolog-based translators. For example, we talk about Prolog procedures that "visit" a node of the parse tree, and we discuss how Prolog procedures evaluate "attributes" of the tree. This is because the literature that discusses Prolog-based translators relates techniques similar to syntax-directed methods, and there is a very straightforward mapping between visiting a child node (using AGs) and calling a Prolog procedure to recursively traverse a substructure representing a subtree, etc. See [61, 58, 15, 2].

Expressing translations using Prolog is a new unproven technology. Most of the discussion in the literature using Prolog for this purpose ([61, 15, 58]) illustrates fairly trivial examples. It is not clear how to express more complicated translations, especially if efficiency is of concern. For example, most translations require several visits to nodes of the parse tree in order to synthesize the translation; i.e., given some inputs to a subtree, only some of its outputs can be calculated. The computation of the remaining outputs is deferred until more of the inputs are known. Using AGs, this presents no problem: at compiler-generation time, the AG compiler compiler figures out for which types of nodes multiple visits are required and generates a compiler that visits these nodes several times (in an optimal fashion). It is not at all clear from the written accounts how Prolog would deal with this situation; examples in the literature only express translations that require a single pass over the tree, or multiple passes in which the programmer explicitly encodes what computation is to be performed during each pass. There are 3 alternatives on how to use Prolog to achieve the same effect as multiple visits found in AGs: (i) Create Prolog procedures which mimic multiple visits by allowing it to "guess" those outputs which cannot yet be computed. This would cause an intolerable amount of backtracking and is clearly not feasible. (ii) Defer evaluation of attributes that cannot yet be computed using Prologs unification methodology; i.e., if a node cannot yet compute an attribute value, a logic variable is created standing for the value of that attribute. When the information to compute the variable becomes available (somewhere else in the tree) , Prolog's unification mechanism would automatically fill in the value. Although this methodology cannot be used in general, it can sometimes be a very powerful technique (e.g., see Warren's [61] usage of the dictionary). (iii) Create Prolog procedures that visit "subtrees" multiple times, just as AGs do. I.e., given a Prolog structure, multiple procedure invocations are made to each substructure. On each subsequent "visit", different parameters are passed to communicate more recently computed information, enabling more "attributes" to get evaluated. The problem with this methodology is that the programmer must explicitly encode how this is to be done, in contrast to AGs where the compiler compiler automatically creates such procedures, based upon attribute dependency analysis. Furthermore, if a node needs a value that was computed on a previous visit, it must recompute this value, as Prolog cannot store state information in the nodes of the tree as can be done in AGs. (It is interesting to note the similarity between this last suggestion and Katayama's [39] AG evaluation strategy). Although this last suggestion is the most feasible, it still requires much more effort and will be far less efficient than using AGs. A different approach, discussed in [2], is to actually implement an AG-like translation methodology in Prolog. In this work, syntax and semantics are specified separately, and semantic functions are written in Prolog. Using Prolog in this respect can create powerful AG-like translators. Unfortunately, because these translators separate syntax and semantics, they do not benefit from the reversibility of Prolog functions, and in order to invert such translations one needs to know how to invert AGs- the subject of this thesis.

Other translation tasks are also difficult to express in Prolog; e.g., negation of a predicate P(x), where the domain of x is infinite. Even more fundamental to the issue of efficiency is the fact that Prolog programs make heavy use of backtracking. Unambiguous AGs require no backtracking whatsoever, as all computation is deterministic[5]. This makes AGs a much more efficient vehicle to express computations than Prolog. Furthermore, the storage requirements of Prolog translators inhibit their usage for large applications, unless some "impure" Prolog code is introduced [61].

Finally, the whole premise that using Prolog to express translations automatically gains invertibility is simply not true. In the words of Cohen [15], "although this is in principle feasible, the use of 'impure' Prolog features such as cut and the assignment (*is*) render the reverse execution impossible." The fact that not all logic program are invertible was actually the subject of an interesting paper by Sickel [55] (where it was also pointed out that for some logic programs there exists very efficient implementations in one direction but not in the other). To restrict Prolog to only reversible functions would severely hamper ones ability to write translations. Furthermore, Cohen himself suggests incorporating more control structures into Prolog to improve its efficiency, which would even further increase the number of nonreversible Prolog constructs in the language. For instance, he suggests having the programmer supply mode declarations, listing each procedure parameter as either an input or an output. This makes Prolog functions look amazingly similar to attribute grammars, but it also removes the basis of reversibility in Prolog. Another work by Shoham and McDermott [54] once again acknowleges the difficulty of inverting Prolog programs. Some of their ideas are similar to our own. For example, one of their algorithms for inverting Prolog programs equips the Prolog interpreter with knowledge on how to invert specific Prolog constructs. This is very similar to our formation of invertive token permuting in section 5.2.

---

[5]In section 7.1 we discuss how to deal with ambiguous AGs, and suggest an algorithm which does entail some backtracking (see also [66]). However even here we are able to do better than Prolog in that we can make use of previously stored intermediate results (attributes) and can perform the backtracking in a more intelligent fashion. This is because, in contrast to Prolog's completely general backtracking mechanism, backtracking for ambiguous AGs is controlled by the structure of the parse tree and attribute dependencies.

Despite these shortcomings, as more experience is gained using Prolog-based translators and Prolog compilers become more efficient, it would be interesting to investigate the issue of invertibility in Prolog (a start in this direction is Sickel's paper [55] quoted above). It would also be interesting to relate the work contained in this thesis to logic programming and Prolog. Although we have stuck to the AG formalism throughout the thesis, it may be the case that the implementation of some of our algorithms becomes simpler using Prolog. For example, the tree unification algorithm of chapter 4 can probably be made alot simpler using Prolog's built in unification algorithm. In concluding our discussion of the relationship between this thesis and Prolog, let us say that although this thesis is based upon AGs, many of its lessons carry over to the Prolog world. This is because this thesis investigates what is easy and what is hard in inverting translations, and to a large extent this is independent of the implementation methodology.

Although not directly related to AG inversion, this thesis has been influenced by research concerning grammar based translation methodologies in general and attribute grammars in particular. The basic principle behind AG-inversion, interpreting certain semantic rules of an AG as themselves being context-free rules of another AG, is similar to efforts described in [23, 25] to compose two AGs rather than invert one. Some technical similarities to this and other works will be found throughout the thesis (see section 4.2).

The third topic discussed in this thesis is source-to-source translators. In contrast to attribute grammar inversion, techniques for constructing these translators have been widely discussed in the literature. Besides the use of attribute grammar inversion, the methodology advocated in this thesis calls for the creation of a canonical form in which to represent all source language programs. Proper design of the canonical form is crucial to the success of this task. Chapter 6 discusses what the canonical form should look like. This research has much in common with the construction of Ada-to-Pascal and Pascal-to-Ada translators described in [3, 41], and later research based upon this approach [10].

1.4. Overview of thesis

This chapter presented some of the motivations to AG inversion and a brief summary of the thesis. The rest of the thesis can be roughly divided into two parts. The first part discusses the technique of attribute grammar inversion. A good portion of this material involves proving the correctness of the technique and elaborating upon the theoretical aspects of inversion. The second part reports on a real system, called INVERT, used to invert attribute grammars and describes how this system can be used to produce source-to-source translators.

Part one consists of chapters 2, 3, and 4. In chapter 2 RIFs are introduced and it is shown how they fit into the broader framework of grammar based translation methodologies. In comparing RIFs to attribute grammars and syntax-directed translation schema, it is shown that RIFs are equivalent in power to attribute grammars. Chapter 3 discusses the central theme of the thesis, the automatic inversion of RIFs. This chapter contains the inversion algorithm and examines properties of the generated inverse in respect to the original RIF. Chapter 4 expands on the theory of attribute grammar inversion, generalizing the ideas behind RIFs.

Part two of the thesis consists of chapters 5, 6, and 7. In chapter 5 the INVERT system is reviewed. Although this system implements the basic inversion algorithm of part one, it also includes many extensions to RIFs that were found to be useful in practice. Chapter 6 relates a methodology for building source-to-source translators based on attribute grammar inversion and a canonical form in which to represent programs. It will emphasize the basic principles that should guide the construction of the canonical form. Chapter 6 also discusses how this methodology of source-to-source translation was used, together with the INVERT system, to construct translators between the Pascal and C programming languages. Chapter 7 summarizes the approach to source-to-source translation presented in this thesis and draws some conclusions about its strengths and weaknesses. These conclusions are used to suggest directions for future research.

This thesis also contains two appendixes. The first shows that AGs, as defined in chapter 2, are extremely general computational devices. They are so general, in fact, that they can define uncomputable translations! The second appendix presents some sample translations between Pascal and C programs, generated by the Pascal-to-C and C-to-Pascal translators discussed in 6.

Chapter 2

Grammar based translation methodologies and RIFs

Grammar based translation methodologies describe a translation using a two stage process. The first stage performs syntactic analysis on the source string. The output of this stage is a *parse tree*, which identifies the syntactic components of the input string. The second stage performs semantic analysis. It takes the parse tree and converts it to a *semantic tree*. A semantic tree is a parse tree decorated with semantic values (attributes). After this process is completed, the translation of the input string will reside in the root of the semantic tree. A grammar based translation methodology formally specifies the syntactic and semantic stages.

The syntactic stage in a grammar based translation methodology is specified by a context-free grammar. This grammar describes the source language (the domain) of the grammar based translation methodology. Using the context-free grammar, one can parse any source string and produce a parse tree. (Parsing strategies for context-free grammars are discussed in [4]). The syntactic stage suffices to recognize valid input strings. In order to specify a translation on these strings, a semantic stage is required. In a grammar based translation methodology, the semantic stage is specified by augmenting the context-free grammar with attributes and semantic functions. After a parse tree for a given input is built according to the context-free grammar, attribute fields are added to nodes in the tree labeled by nonterminal symbols. The translation is accomplished by "filling in" these attribute fields according to the rules specified in the semantic functions. Since semantic functions express the value of attributes in terms of other attributes, an attribute field cannot be evaluated until all the attribute fields upon which it depends have been evaluated. The translation of the input string is the value of a distinguished attribute of the root.

Grammar based translation methodologies differ from one another according to the restrictions they place on attributes and semantic functions. Two of the most well known grammar based translation methodologies, attribute grammars and syntax-directed translation schema, illustrate this point. Whereas a syntax-directed translation scheme can perform only simple translations, an attribute grammar can be written for any computable translation problem. The next section reviews attribute grammars and syntax-directed translation schema. After this a new grammar based translation methodology, Restricted Inverse Form (RIF) grammars, is introduced. RIFs lie between attribute grammars and syntax-directed translation schema in generality; i.e., any syntax-directed translation schema is a RIF and any RIF is an attribute grammar. RIFs, as shown in the next chapter, are special in that they can be easily inverted to specify the inverse translation. Section 2.2 takes a closer look at the grammar based translation methodology hierarchy and shows the surprising result that any translation expressible by an attribute grammar can be expressed by a RIF.

Before proceeding to discuss the various grammar based translation methodologies, we need to make precise the notion of a translation. A *translation* is a subset of $\Sigma^* \times \Delta^*$ for finite alphabets Σ and Δ. In such a case we say that the translation *is over* $\Sigma \times \Delta$. The *domain* of a translation T, denoted *Dom(T)*, is $\{w \mid$ for some x, (w,x) is in T$\}$. The *range* of T is $\{x \mid$ for some w, (w,x) is in T$\}$. If T is a translation such that (w,x) in T and (w',x) in T implies that $w = w'$ then T is said to be *uniquely invertible*. If (w,x) in T and (w,x') in T implies that $x = x'$ than T is said to be a *function*. A uniquely invertible function T is *one-to-one (1-1)*. If T is not uniquely invertible then it is *many-to-one* and if T is not a function then it is *one-to-many*.

2.1. Grammar based translation methodologies

2.1.1. Attribute Grammars

Attribute grammars were first proposed by Knuth [43] as a way to specify the semantics of context-free languages[6]. The basis of an attribute grammar is a context-free grammar. This describes the context-free language that is the domain of the translation; i.e., those strings on which the translation is defined. This context-free grammar is augmented with *attributes* and *semantic functions*. Attributes are associated with the nonterminal symbols of the grammar. We write "X.A" to denote attribute A of symbol X, and $A(X)$ to denote the set of attributes associated with X. Semantic functions are associated with productions; they describe how the values of some attributes of the production are defined in terms of the values of other attributes of the production. Given a production $[p: X_0 ::= \alpha_0 X_1 \alpha_1 X_2 ... X_{n_p} \alpha_{n_p}]$, we call $A(p) = A(X_0) \cup ... \cup A(X_{n_p})$ the attributes of p. (Throughout this thesis, α_i represent terminal strings and X_i represent nonterminal symbols).

Figure 2-1 gives an attribute grammar that describes binary numerals and the integer values they denote. In this attribute grammar there are 5 productions and each production has associated attributes and semantic functions. In production p_2, <digits0> and <digits1> denote separate occurrences of the same symbol, <digits>; the numeric suffixes distinguish these different occurrences.

A semantic function specifies the value of an attribute-occurrence of the production, e.g. the value of digits0.val in production 2 of figure 2-1 is defined to be equal to the sum of digits1.val and digit.val. Semantic functions are pure functions, they have no side-effects. Their only arguments are either constants or other attribute-occurrences of the production.

---

[6]A formal definition of AGs is presented in section 2.1.1.1. The reader already familiar with AGs may want to skip the following primer on AGs and jump to that section.

Context free symbols of the attribute grammar and their attributes:

binary_number: { binary_number.val }
digits: { digits.val, digits.place }
digit: { digit.val, digit.place }
1: ∅
0: ∅

Productions of the attribute grammar and their semantic functions:

p1: binary_number ::= digits.
    binary_num.val = digits.val;
    digits.place = 0;

p2: digits0 ::= digits1 digit.
    digits0.val = digits1.val + digit.val;
    digit.place = digits0.place;
    digits1.place = digits0.place + 1;

p3: digits ::= digit.
    digits.val = digit.val;
    digit.place = digits.place;

p4: digit ::= 0.
    digit.val = 0;

p5: digit ::= 1.
    digit.val = $2^{\text{digit.place}}$;

Figure 2-1: An attribute grammar

How an attribute grammar specifies a translation can be most easily explained by an operational description. The underlying context-free grammar of an attribute grammar describes a language. Any string in this language has a parse tree associated with it by the grammar. The nodes of this parse tree can be labeled with symbols of the grammar. Each interior node of this tree, N, has two productions associated with it. The left-part production (LP) is the production that applies at N, say p, deriving N's children. The right-part production (RP) is the production that applies at the parent of N, say p', deriving N and its siblings. Leaves of the tree don't have LP productions; the root doesn't have a RP production.

A *semantic tree* is a parse tree in which each node contains fields that correspond to the attributes of its labelling grammar symbol. Each of these fields is an

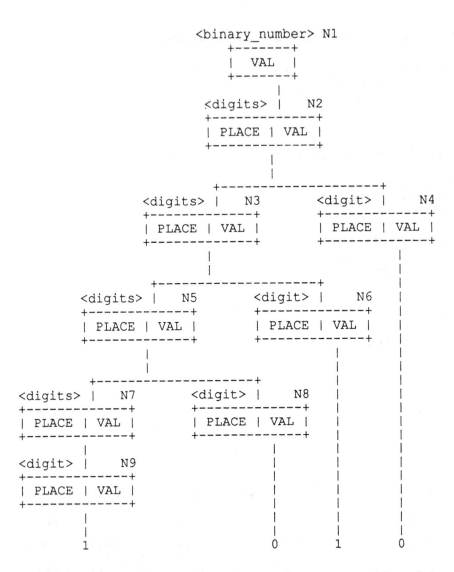

Figure 2-2: A semantic tree for the attribute grammar of figure 2-1

attribute-instance. Associated with each attribute is a set of possible values that instances of this attribute can be assigned. This is analogous to the "type" of a variable in a programming language. However, each attribute-instance takes on precisely one such value; attribute-instances <u>are not variables</u>. The values of attribute-instances are specified by the semantic functions. Figure 2-2 shows a semantic tree for the string 1010 of the attribute grammar given in figure 2-1. Each node in this tree is labelled with its associated grammar symbol. To distinguish between different instances of the same grammar symbol each node is also assigned a number.

The semantic functions of a production represent a template for specifying the values of attribute-instances in the semantic tree. Consider figure 2-2 again. N2 is a semantic tree node labeled by the context-free symbol <digits>. It has two productions associated with it: [p_1: binary_number ::= digits] (its RP production) and [p_2: digits0 ::= digits1 digit] (its LP production). The semantic function <digits.place = 0> of production p_1 indicates that the value of attribute-instance N2.place will be set equal to the constant 0. Similarly, the semantic function <binary_number.val = digits.val> of that production indicates that the value of attribute-instance N1.VAL should be copied from the value of N2.val.

Since two different productions are associated with each attribute-instance, there could be two semantic functions that independently specify its value, one from the LP production and one from the RP production. If we assume that each attribute-instance is defined by only one semantic function, either from the LP production or from the RP production, then we must guard against an attribute-instance not being defined at all because the LP production assumed that the RP production would define it and vice versa. These difficulties are avoided in attribute grammars by adopting the convention that for every attribute, X.A, either: (1) every instance of X.A is defined by a semantic function associated with its LP production, or (2) every instance of X.A is defined by a semantic function associated with its RP production. Attributes whose instances are all defined in their LP production are called *synthesized* attributes; attributes whose instances are all defined in their RP production are called *inherited* attributes. Every attribute is either inherited or synthesized. Inherited attributes propagate information down the tree, towards the leaves. Synthesized attributes propagate information up the tree, toward the root. The start symbol has no inherited attributes. From the point of view of an individual production the above conditions require that the semantic functions of a production MUST define EXACTLY all the inherited attributes of the right-part symbols and all synthesized attributes of the left-part symbol.

Thus the semantic functions of an attribute grammar specify a unique value for each attribute-instance. However, in order to actually compute the value of attribute-instance X.att we must first have available the values of those other attribute-instances that are arguments of the semantic function that defines X.att. In the example of figure 2-2, before N1.VAL can be computed the value of N2.VAL must have already been computed. Such *dependency relations* restrict the order in which attribute-instances can be evaluated. In extreme cases an attribute-instance can depend on itself; such a situation is called a circularity and by definition such situations are forbidden from occurring in well-defined attribute grammars. In general, it is an exponentially hard problem [30] to determine that an attribute grammar is *non-circular*; i.e. that no semantic tree that can be generated by the attribute grammar contains a circularly defined attribute-instance. Fortunately there are several interesting and widely applicable sufficient conditions that can be checked in polynomial time [12, 31, 37, 42].

The result of the translation specified by an attribute grammar is realized as the value of a distinguished (necessarily synthesized) attribute-instance of the root of the semantic tree. In order to compute this value the other attribute-instances must be computed. Since the evaluator must be capable of evaluating *any* semantic tree of the grammar G, embodied in its control structure must be some general mechanism describing how to evaluate semantic trees. An *attribute grammar evaluator strategy* describes how to build the control structure of an evaluator. It is a meta-algorithm for building an algorithm that will compute attribute-instances in an order such that no attribute-instance is computed before all dependent attribute-instances are available and such that the distinguished attribute-instance of the root is computed. An attribute grammar evaluator strategy may work correctly only on a subset of all well-defined attribute grammars, but it must work correctly on any semantic tree of an acceptable attribute grammar. Many attribute grammar evaluator strategies have been considered [64] and many compiler compilers based on AGs have been constructed [51, 24, 38, 18]. While past research has been successful in generating time efficient evaluators, current research focuses on building space efficient evaluators as well [56, 21].

2.1.1.1. A formal definition of AGs

Let Σ and Δ be two finite alphabets. An AG specifying a translation $\Sigma \times \Delta$ is a 4-tuple (G, A, VAL, SF). G is a context-free grammar (N, Σ, S, P), where N is the set of nonterminals, Σ is the set of terminals, S is the start symbol, and P is the set of productions.

A is the set of attributes. Each attribute $a \in A$ is of the form X.a, indicating that a is an attribute associated with the nonterminal X. Each attribute $a \in A$ is also marked *inherited* or *synthesized*. The start symbol S can only have synthesized attributes and it must have at least one distinguished synthesized attribute S.value.

VAL is a function mapping each attribute a in A to a set of possible values VAL(a). $VAL(S.value) \subseteq \{v \mid v \in \Delta^*\}$.

SF is a set of *semantic functions*, where each $f \in SF$ is associated with some production $p \in P$. If $f \in SF$ is associated with [p: $X_0 ::= \alpha_0 X_1 \alpha_1 X_2 ... X_{n_p} \alpha_{n_p}$], then f is of the form: $X_{i_1}.a_1 = g(X_{i_2}.a_2,...,X_{i_r}.a_r)$, where g is a mapping from $VAL(X_{i_2}.a_2) \times ... \times VAL(X_{i_r}.a_r)$ to $VAL(X_{i_1}.a_1)$, i_j $(1 \leq j \leq r)$ is in $[1..n_p]$, and each $X_{i_j}.a_{1_j}$ is in the set of attributes A. There exists exactly one semantic function in SF computing each synthesized attribute of X_0 in p and each inherited attribute of X_i $(1 \leq i \leq n_p)$ in p.

Given a parse tree PT in G, there is an associated semantic tree which is obtained by assigning attribute values to nodes in PT. Let N be a node in PT labeled X. Then N will have a attribute value N.a associated with it for each attribute X.a in A. Let N be the root of an occurrence of the production [p: $X_0 ::= \alpha_0 X_1 \alpha_1 X_2 ... X_{n_p} \alpha_{n_p}$]. If X has a synthesized attribute X.a associated with it, then there exists a semantic function f in SF associated with p which defines X.a. The function f is of the form: $X.a = g(X_{i_2}.a_2,...,X_{i_r}.a_r)$. N.a gets assigned a value $g(N_{i_2}.a_2,...,N_{i_r}.a_r)$, where N_0 indicates the node N and, for $i > 0$, N_i is the ith (nonterminal) son of N. This assumes that each $N_{i_j}.a_j$ $(2 \leq j \leq r)$ has a unique value. Otherwise N.a is undefined. (If these rules of assigning values creates a circularity, then all the attribute values in that circular definition will be undefined). Similarly, for each child N_i ($1 \leq i \leq n_p$) of N, if X_i has an inherited attribute associated with it, then there exists a semantic function f in SF defining X.a. The function f is of the form: $X_i.a = g(X_{i_2}.a_2,...,X_{i_r}.a_r)$. $N_i.a$ gets the value $g(N_{i_2}.a_2,...,N_{i_r}.a_r)$. Once again, if $N_{i_j}.a_j$ is not uniquely defined then $N_i.a$ is undefined.

The translation T defined by an AG are those pairs (w, x) such that
1. there exists a parse tree PT in G for w, and
2. in the semantic tree obtained from PT, the root node attribute R.value equals x. (R is labeled by the nonterminal S).

2.1.1.2. Translations defined as ERROR

In order to allow attribute grammars to compute translations over non-context-free domains, we introduce the special symbol ERROR. If T is a translation over $\Sigma \times \Delta$, then ERROR is a symbol not in Δ. To specify a translation over a non-context-free domain, a "covering" context-free language is used which contains the domain of the translation. Those strings which are in the covering language but not in the domain of the translation are "translated" to the distinguished symbol ERROR. According to this convention, a translation specified by an attribute grammar (or any grammar based translation methodology) are those pairs (w,x) computed by some semantic tree, where x ≠ ERROR. Hence, given an attribute grammar with an ambiguous underlying context-free grammar, to determine whether or not a string w is in the domain of the translation, all parse trees for w must be built and the corresponding semantic trees must be evaluated. The string w is in the domain of the translation if and only if one of these semantic trees translates w to x ≠ ERROR. Using this definition, two grammar based translation methodologies G and G′ can specify the same translation even if G gives rise to a semantic tree "translating" w to ERROR and G′ does not contain such a semantic tree. Unless we explicitly specify to the contrary, the term attribute grammar will mean attribute grammars allowing ERROR translations as defined here. The use of ERROR is similar to the concept of *deviant evaluations* found in [46].

Although the use of ERROR allows AGs to define translations over non-context-free domains, it does have some drawbacks. In appendix A it is shown that for an arbitrary

AG G expressing the translation T, it is not, in general, decidable whether or not (x, w) ∈ T. However, if we restrict AGs so that for any input at most a finite number of parses are produced, then AGs once again become computable. Since this restriction is very reasonable in practice, our use of ERROR should not pose any problems for real systems.

2.1.2. Syntax-Directed Translation Schema

Syntax-directed translation schema were first defined by Irons [29] and subsequently investigated by several researchers [5, 6]. A syntax-directed translation scheme, like an attribute grammar, defines the translation using a context-free grammar. Yet they differ sharply from one another in philosophy. Attribute grammars have little to say about what operations can be performed in the translation process; the only restrictions they place on semantic functions concerns circularity requirements. A syntax-directed translation scheme, on the other hand, formalizes all aspects of the translation process, rigorously defining the operations permitted by semantic functions. This additional rigor has advantages and disadvantages. Because all the constructs used in a syntax-directed translation scheme are well understood, the specification of syntax directed translations can be formally analyzed, automatically checked for errors, and verified in respect to an external specification to a much greater degree than attribute grammars. Yet, these restrictions also limit the type of translations that can be described by syntax-directed translation schema [5, 6], making them an impractical tool for real translator-writing systems.

Although syntax-directed translation schema are usually defined in terms of permutations of parse trees [8], in order to show their relationship to other grammar based translation methodologies we describe them as a restricted form of attribute grammars. Before proceeding, we need the following definition, which will play an important role in the rest of the thesis. A function f is a *token permuting function* over an alphabet Δ if and only if it is of the form: $f(\delta_1,...,\delta_n) = $ Concatenate$(\beta_0, \delta_{i_1}, \beta_1, \delta_{i_2},...,\delta_{i_n}, \beta_n)$, where each $\delta_k \in \Delta^*$ $(1 \le k \le n)$, $[i_1...i_n]$ is a permutation of [1..n], and each β_k ($1 \leq k \leq n$) is a constant in Δ^*. The *constant token permuting function* f() returns a constant string in Δ^*.

The function f is called a *token permuting function* as it permutes the order of its arguments and inserts constant tokens of Δ in between them.   It is important to emphasize that <u>a token permuting function cannot delete any of its arguments</u>; they must all appear exactly once on the right hand side of the equation. Less restricted versions of token permuting functions are given in chapter 5.

Let Σ and Δ be two finite alphabets. A *syntax-directed translation scheme* defining the translation T over $\Sigma \times \Delta$ is an attribute grammar obeying the following restrictions:

1. Each nonterminal symbol X of the underlying context-free grammar has exactly one synthesized attribute X.trans and no inherited attributes. X.trans will take on values in Δ^*.

2. Each production [p: $X_0 ::= \alpha_0 X_1 \alpha_1 X_2 \ldots X_{n_p} \alpha_{n_p}$] ($\alpha_i \in \Sigma^*$, X_i is a nonterminal of the underlying context-free grammar) has exactly one semantic function f defining X_0.trans where f is a token permuting function over Δ of the form $f(X_1.\text{trans},\ldots,X_{n_p}.\text{trans})$.[7]

3. The value of the translation is specified to be the value of the trans attribute of the root (S.trans).

Figure 2-3 gives a syntax-directed translation scheme translating simple English descriptions of mathematical expressions into post-fix notation. For example, it will translate the English phrase 'multiply 5.7 and 8' into the post-fix Polish expression '(5.7,8,*)' and the phrase 'add 5 and 9' into '(5,9,+)'.

---

[7]In the case that p has no nonterminals on the right hand side of the production then X_0 is defined by a constant token permuting function f(), returning a constant string.

p_1: S ::= Op Number1 and Number2.
    S.trans = Concatenate('(', Number1.trans, ',', Number2.trans,
                        ',', Op.trans, ')');
p_2: Number ::= Integer.
    Number.trans = Integer.trans;

p_3: Number ::= Decimal_num.
    Number.trans = Decimal_num.trans;

p_4: Op ::= add.
    Op.trans = '+';

p_5: Op ::= multiply.
    Op.trans = '*';

p_6: Integer ::= digits.
    Integer.trans = digits.trans;

p_7: Decimal_num ::= digits1 . digits2.
    Decimal_num.trans = Concatenate(digits1.trans, '.', digits2.trans);

Figure 2-3: A syntax-directed translation scheme

2.1.3. RIFs

This section introduces RIFs. These grammars can be viewed as a restricted form of attribute grammars or as a generalized version of syntax-directed translation schema. Like the latter, they make use of token permuting functions as the fundamental operation at a node of the semantic tree. Like the former, however, they make extensive use of arbitrary attributes to transport context-sensitive information around the tree, allowing more general translations than syntax-directed translation schema.

Let $\delta_k \in \Delta^* \cup \{ \text{ERROR} \}$ $(1 \leq k \leq n)$, and let $\text{ERROR}(\delta_1,...,\delta_n) = $ if $(\delta_1 = \text{ERROR})$ or ... or $(\delta_n = \text{ERROR})$ then true else false. The definition of RIFs relies upon a generalized version of token permuting functions. A function f is a *token permuting clause* over an alphabet Δ if and only if it is of the following form:

$f(\delta_1,...,\delta_n; arg_1,...,arg_{s-1}) =$

    if $\text{ERROR}(\delta_1,...,\delta_n)$ or $g_1(arg_1)$ then **ERROR**

    elsif $g_2(arg_2)$ then $f_2(\delta_1,...,\delta_n)$

elsif $g_3(arg_3)$ then $f_3(\delta_1,...,\delta_n)$

.
.
.

elsif $g_{s-1}(arg_{s-1})$ then $f_{s-1}(\delta_1,...,\delta_n)$

else $f_s(\delta_1,...,\delta_n)$

where each g_j $(1 \leq j \leq s-1)$ is an arbitrary boolean function and each f_j $(2 \leq j \leq s)$ is a token permuting function over Δ.

A token permuting clause is more powerful than a token permuting function in two ways. First of all, it sometimes returns the value ERROR, which a token permuting function cannot. Secondly, even when it returns a value other than ERROR, it can choose from among a finite number of token permuting functions to compute this value. Which function it chooses is based upon the evaluation of the g_j boolean conditions. The arguments to a token permuting clause fall into two classes. The first class contains the δ_k $(1 \leq k \leq n)$ "string" arguments, each taking on values in $\Delta^* \cup \{$ ERROR $\}$. The second class contains the arg_j $(1 \leq j \leq s-1)$ "control" variables, which have no special structure.

Let Σ and Δ be two finite alphabets. A RIF defining the translation T over $\Sigma \times \Delta$ is an attribute grammar obeying the following restrictions:

1. Each nonterminal X has a distinguished synthesized attribute X.trans taking on values in $\Delta^* \cup \{$ERROR$\}$. X.trans represents the translation of the substring which X derives.

2. For each production [p: $X_0 ::= \alpha_0 X_1 \alpha_1 X_2 ... X_{n_p} \alpha_{n_p}$] the semantic function defining X_0.trans is a token permuting clause of the form $f(X_1.trans,...,X_{n_p}.trans; atts_1,...,atts_{s-1})$ where each $atts_j$ $(1 \leq j \leq s-1)$ is a subset of A(p). Note that the "string" arguments to each f are exactly the trans attributes of the production's right-part nonterminals and the "control" arguments are subsets of arbitrary attributes of the production.

3. The value of the translation is specified to be the value of the trans attribute of the root (S.trans).

A RIF is like a syntax-directed translation scheme in that each nonterminal has a special synthesized attribute (the trans attribute) which stores the translation of its subtree and which is usually defined by a token permuting function. But a RIF surpasses a syntax-directed translation scheme in expressive power not only in that it allows the trans attribute to be assigned the value ERROR, but in that it allows other attributes to be associated with nonterminals. These "other" attributes influence the translation by determining which token permuting function is chosen to evaluate the trans attribute (they serve as arguments to the g_j boolean expressions). This allows RIFs to express context sensitive translations, something syntax-directed translation schema cannot do. For example, figure 2-4 gives a RIF which accepts strings of the form '$a^i\, b^j\, c^k$' and translates them to 'OK $a^i\, b^j\, c^k$' if $i = j = k$, and to 'NOT OK $a^i\, b^j\, c^k$' otherwise. This language cannot be expressed by any syntax-directed translation schema, since the target language is not context-free.

Since every token permuting clause is of the form:

if ERROR($Y_1,...,Y_n$) or $g_1(arg_1)$ then ERROR

elsif $g_2(arg_2)$ then $f_2(Y_1,...,Y_n)$

elsif $g_3(arg_3)$ then $f_3(Y_1,...,Y_n)$

.
.
.

elsif $g_{s-1}(arg_{s-1})$ then $f_{s-1}(Y_1,...,Y_n)$

else $f_s(Y_1,...,Y_n)$,

if for any node N in any semantic tree N.trans = ERROR, the result of the translation will be ERROR. To ease our notational burden, we can omit the clause ERROR($Y_1,...,Y_n$) and write all token permuting clauses of the above form as:

if $g_1(arg_1)$ then ERROR

elsif $g_2(arg_2)$ then $f_2(Y_1,...,Y_n)$

elsif $g_3(arg_3)$ then $f_3(Y_1,...,Y_n)$

.
.
.

elsif $g_{s-1}(arg_{s-1})$ then $f_{s-1}(Y_1,...,Y_n)$

else $f_s(Y_1,...,Y_n)$,

instead. To accommodate this relaxed notation, we need to revise our definition of token permuting functions so that if any string argument to a token permuting function is ERROR, then the function returns the value ERROR.

p_1: S ::= A B C.
    S.trans = if (A.number = B.number = C.number)
        then Concatenate('OK', A.trans, B.trans, C.trans)
        else Concatenate('NOT OK', A.trans, B.trans, C.trans);

p_2: A0 ::= a A1.
    A0.trans = Concatenate('a', A1.trans);
    A0.number = A1.number + 1;

p_3: A ::= a.
    A.trans = 'a';
    A.number = 1;

p_4: B0 ::= b B1.
    B0.trans = Concatenate('b', B1.trans);
    B0.number = B1.number + 1;

p_5: B ::= b.
    B.trans = 'b';
    B.number = 1;

p_6: C0 ::= c C1.
    C0.trans = Concatenate('c', C1.trans);
    C0.number = C1.number + 1;

p_7: C ::= c.
    C.trans = 'c';
    C.number = 1;

Figure 2-4: A RIF

To illustrate the increased expressive power of RIFs over syntax-directed translation schema in a more natural setting, figure 2-5 presents a RIF which generalizes the syntax-directed translation scheme of figure 2-3 by taking type information into consideration. In particular, it will translate the English phrase 'multiply 5.7 by 8' into the post-fix Polish expression '(5.7,8,$*_r$)', where $*_r$ indicates real multiplication, and the English phrase 'Add 3 to 4' into the expression '(3,4,$+_i$)', where $+_i$ indicates integer addition[8]. Note that the semantics of productions p_1 and p_2 enforce proper usage of the prepositions 'by' and 'to', causing incorrect usages to return the value ERROR.

---

[8]Although in this particular case a syntax-directed translation scheme could be devised to implement the same translation, the RIF is a more natural way of expressing it. This is because a syntax-directed translation scheme would need to duplicate context-free productions, one set for real operations and another set for integer operations. In the RIF, type information is taken care of at the semantic and not syntactic level.

p_1: S ::= Op Number1 by Number2.
    Op.type = If (Number1.type = decimal_pt) or
        (Number2.type = decimal_pt)
      then decimal_pt else int;
    S.trans = if (Op.trans='+$_r$') or (Op.trans='+$_i$') then ERROR
        else Concatenate('(',Number1.trans, ',', Number2.trans,
            ',', Op.trans, ')');
p_2: S ::= Op Number1 to Number2.
    Op.type = If (Number1.type = decimal_pt) or
        (Number2.type = decimal_pt)
      then decimal_pt else int;
    S.trans = if (Op.trans='*$_r$') or (Op.trans='*$_i$') then ERROR
        else Concatenate('(',Number1.trans, ',', Number2.trans,
            ',', Op.trans, ')');
p_3: Number ::= Integer.
    Number.type = int;
    Number.trans = Integer.trans;

p_4: Number ::= Decimal_num.
    Number.type = decimal_pt;
    Number.trans = Decimal_num.trans;

p_5: Op ::= add.
    Op.trans = If (Op.type = decimal_pt) then '+$_r$' else '+$_i$';

p_6: Op ::= multiply.
    Op.trans = If (Op.type = decimal_pt) then '*$_r$' else '*$_i$';

p_7: Integer ::= digits.
    Integer.trans = digits.trans;

p_8: Decimal_num ::= digits1 . digits2.
    Decimal_num.trans = Concatenate(digits1.trans,'.',digits2.trans);

Figure 2-5: A RIF using type information

RIFs are especially interesting because they display a duality between syntax and semantics. For any production [p: X_0 ::= X_1 ⋯ X_{n_p}], X_0 can be viewed as generating the strings derived from its children, X_1, ..., X_{n_p}. On the other hand, X_0 synthesizes its translation by permuting and concatenating the trans attributes of these children. The next chapter will show how to exploit this duality for purposes of inversion. In essence, RIFs enforce an isomorphic structure between the context-free grammar describing the domain of the translation and the context-free grammar describing the range of the translation. This allows one to recover the parse of the domain element from the parse of the range element.

2.2. The equivalence of RIFs and Attribute Grammars

This section demonstrates that RIFs are equivalent in computational power to attribute grammars by showing how to convert an arbitrary attribute grammar G to a RIF G' computing the same translation. The construction of G' from G is quite simple. Say that G translates w to x. On input w, G' will simulate G exactly, producing the translation x in the root node. This computation of x, however, may not have been done using token permuting functions. Therefore, in order to make G' into a RIF, x is sent back done the tree, all the way to the leaf nodes. The ith leaf node, using a token permuting clause, "picks off" the ith symbol in x. The translation x is reassembled by synthesizing the leaf values up the tree and concatenating them, using token permuting functions. In this way the value of x will percolate up the tree, once again arriving at the root node. The only difficulty with this construction is when the length of x is greater than the number of leaf nodes in the tree. To get around this problem, extra leafs nodes are obtained using ε-productions. A formal description of this construction follows.

Let Σ and Δ be finite alphabets, where $\Delta = \{ \gamma_1, ..., \gamma_m \}$. Let G be any attribute grammar defining a translation T over $\Sigma \times \Delta$ and let the underlying context-free grammar of G be (V, Σ, P, S), where V is the set of nonterminals, Σ the set of terminals, P the set of productions and S the goal symbol. Let S.value be the distinguished attribute of the root. Create the RIF G' from G computing the same translation as follows:

1. Let (V', Σ, P', S') be the underlying context-free grammar of G', where $V' = V \cup \{ S', E \}$ and $P' = P \cup \{ [p_1: S' ::= S E], [p_2: E ::= E E], [p_3: E ::= \varepsilon] \}$.

2. Let each nonterminal X of G', $X \neq S'$ and $X \neq E$, have the same attributes as in G. In addition, let each one of these nonterminals have one additional inherited attribute, X.trans_in, and two additional synthesized attributes, X.trans_out and X.trans. Assign S' one synthesized attribute, S'.trans. Assign E one inherited attribute, E.trans_in, and two synthesized attributes E.trans_out and E.trans. S'.trans will be the distinguished attribute of G'.

3. Let $[p: X_0 ::= \alpha_0 X_1 \alpha_1 X_2 ... X_{n_p} \alpha_{n_p}]$ (X_i a nonterminal of G' and α_i in Σ^*) be a production of G', $p \neq p_1$ (but p can equal p_2), such that the number of nonterminals on the right hand side of the production is ≥ 1. Let p have all the semantic functions as it had in G. In addition, this production needs

semantic functions to define $X_0.\text{trans\_out}$, $X_0.\text{trans}$, and $X_i.\text{trans\_in}$, for $1 \leq i \leq n_p$. To this end, let $X_1.\text{trans\_in} = X_0.\text{trans\_in}$ and $X_{i+1}.\text{trans\_in} = X_i.\text{trans\_out}$, $1 \leq i \leq n_p - 1$. Let $X_0.\text{trans\_out} = X_{n_p}.\text{trans\_out}$ and $X_0.\text{trans} = \text{Concatenate}(X_1.\text{trans},...,X_{n_p}.\text{trans})$. (In the case that $p = p_2$, then these are its only semantic functions).

4. For each production $[p: X ::= \alpha]$ in G', where α is in Σ^*, let p have all the semantic functions as it had in G (p may equal p_3, in which case it will only have the semantic functions about to be listed). In addition, add the semantic functions $X.\text{trans\_out} = \text{AllButFirst}(X.\text{trans\_in})$ and

X.trans = if X.trans_in $\neq \varepsilon$ and

      FIRST(X.trans_in) $\neq$ 'γ_1' and

      FIRST(X.trans_in) $\neq$ 'γ_2' and ...

      FIRST(X.trans_in) $\neq$ 'γ_m'

      then ERROR /* input doesn't belong to input alphabet */

      elsif FIRST(X.trans_in) = 'γ_1' then 'γ_1'

      elsif FIRST(X.trans_in) = 'γ_2' then 'γ_2'

      .
      .
      .

      elsif FIRST(X.trans_in) = 'γ_m' then 'γ_m'

      else ε;

If $w \neq \varepsilon$ then $\text{FIRST}(w)$ returns the first letter of the string w and $\text{AllButFirst}(w)$ returns the string w with the first letter removed. If $w = \varepsilon$ then $\text{FIRST}(w)$ and $\text{AllButFirst}(w)$ return ε.

5. Let $[p_1: S' ::= S\ E]$ have the semantic functions: $<S'.\text{trans} = \text{if}\ (S.\text{value} \neq \text{Concatenate}(S.\text{trans}, E.\text{trans}))$ then ERROR else $\text{Concatenate}(S.\text{trans}, E.\text{trans})>$, $<S.\text{trans\_in} = S.\text{value}>$, and $<E.\text{trans\_in} = S.\text{trans\_out}>$.

Theorem 1: The algorithm given above constructs a RIF G' computing the same translation as the attribute grammar G .

Proof: To prove this theorem, one needs to show that (i) G' is a RIF and (ii) (w, x) is in the translation described by G iff it is in the translation described by G'. That the construction yields a valid RIF G' can be easily seen by checking the produced grammar G' against the definition of RIFs. To see that the two grammars describe the same translation, it suffices to show that for every valid semantic tree in G translating w to x, there exists a valid semantic tree in G' translating w to x, and vice versa.

Let ST be a semantic tree. The set *Nonterm(ST)* are those nonterminal nodes of ST whose children are all terminal nodes. The following shows that if there exists a semantic tree ST translating w to x (x ≠ ERROR) in G, then there exists a semantic tree performing the same translation in G'.

Let $x = x_1,...,x_{|x|}$. Consider the following two possibilities: *Case i:* $|Nonterm(ST)| - |x| \geq 0$. Then let ST' be the semantic tree in G' which is identical to ST except that "attached" to the root ST is the production $[p_1: S' ::= S E]$; i.e., in ST', S' is the root, S and E are its children. Apply production $[p_3: E ::= \varepsilon]$ to the son E of S'. *Case ii:* $|Nonterm(ST)| - |x| < 0$. Obtain the tree ST' in G' by augmenting ST with the production $[p_1: S' ::= S E]$; i.e., connect the root of ST labeled S to S' and add a brother to S labeled E. Repeatedly apply production $[p_2: E ::= E E]$ to the subtree rooted at E until the number of frontier nodes labeled E in that subtree is $= |x| - |Nonterm(ST)|$. Then repeatedly apply production $[p_3: E ::= \varepsilon]$ to each one of these frontier nodes.

In either case i or ii, the resultant tree ST' is a complete semantic tree for G' containing ST as a subtree of its root. The attribute S.value will be computed just as it was in ST and will therefore equal x. Furthermore, the number of nonterminal nodes in *Nonterm(ST')* is $\geq |x|$. One can number these nonterminal nodes consecutively in a left-to-right manner, such that the leftmost node is numbered 1 and every node to the immediate right of a node N is numbered one more than N. This numbering corresponds to the numbering given by the following procedure: initially set the value of a counter to 1. Start at the child of the root labeled S and visit its subtree in a depth-first left-to-right fashion. Upon reaching a node in *Nonterm(ST')*, number it by the value of counter and then increment the counter by one. This is schematically illustrated figure 2-6.

Note that the flow of attribute propagation, starting at the attribute S.trans_in and continuing through trans_in and trans_out attributes, exactly follows the visiting sequence of this procedure, as illustrated in figure 2-7.

Let N be a node in *Nonterm(ST')*. One can establish that the value of the attribute

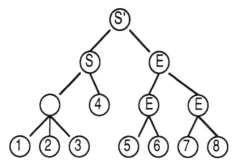

Figure 2-6: Depth-first left-to-right ordering of nodes

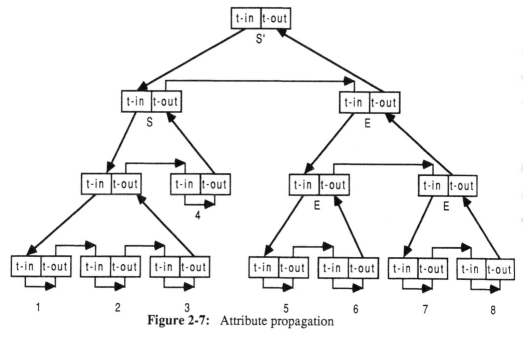

Figure 2-7: Attribute propagation

N.trans, where N is in *Nonterm(ST')* and has number = i, is either = x_i (if $1 \leq i \leq |x|$) or is = ε (if i > |x|). This is because the string x originates at the attribute S.trans_in and then follows the attribute route described above. Call the value that flows along this route Q. Throughout the route the value Q is merely copied over from one attribute to another, except when reaching a node N in *Nonterm(ST')*. Then N.trans gets set to FIRST(Q) if Q ≠ ε and to ε otherwise. Before the value Q proceeds on its journey, it gets truncated by its first letter. Hence, the trans attribute of the ith node in *Nonterm(ST')* gets the ith letter of x as its value, if i≤ |x|, and ε otherwise.

Every nonterminal node in ST', including the root S', has a distinguished trans attribute. The nonterminal nodes in *Nonterm(ST')* have their trans attributes computed as above. Call these trans attributes *primitive*. Every other nonterminal node N has at least one son who is a nonterminal node, and the attribute N.trans is computed by concatenating the trans attributes of its children together. Hence the value of each attribute N.trans in ST' is the concatenation, left-to-right, of the primitive attributes in its subtree. In particular, S'.trans is the concatenation, left-to-right, of all primitive attributes in the tree, and this is simply the value of the string x. Therefore the condition attached to p_1 (computing ERROR) will be false, ST' will be valid, and ST' will compute the same translation as ST.

It now remains to be shown that if there exists a semantic tree ST' translating w to x (x ≠ ERROR) in G', then there exists a semantic tree performing the same translation in G. The production applying at the root of ST' must be p_1, and must therefore have a child labeled by S. The subtree rooted at S is in its own right a semantic tree of G. Furthermore, since the value of S'.trans ≠ ERROR, the condition associated with the token permuting clause of p_1 must evaluate to false. This implies that both S'.trans and S.value must equal the concatenation of S.trans and E.trans. Hence S'.trans equals S.value and the tree rooted at S would be a semantic tree of T computing the same translation as ST'.

For some string w, (w, ERROR) may be computed by a semantic tree in G' but not by a semantic tree in G (for example, if not enough E nodes are included). Nonetheless, since for all x ≠ ERROR, (w, x) is in the translation computed by G' iff it is in the translation computed by G, the translations are equivalent. **End of proof.**

To demonstrate the construction of this theorem, figure 2-8 gives an attribute grammar translating a^i to b^{2^i} and figure 2-9 gives the RIF constructed from this attribute grammar performing the same translation. A typical semantic tree for this RIF is presented in figure 2-10.

p_4: $S_0 ::= S_1$ a
  S_0.value = Concatenate(S_1.value, S_1.value);

p_5: S ::= a
  S.value = 'bb';

Figure 2-8: An attribute grammar translating a^i to b^{2^i}

p_1: S' ::= S E
  S.trans_in = S.value;
  E.trans_in = S.trans_out;
  S'.trans = if S.value ≠ Concatenate(S.trans, E.trans) then **ERROR**
    else Concatenate(S.trans, E.trans);

p_2: $E_0 ::= E_1 E_2$
  E_1.trans_in = E_0.trans_in;
  E_2.trans_in = E_1.trans_out;
  E_0.trans_out = E_2.trans_out;
  E_0.trans = Concatenate(E_1.trans, E_2.trans);

p_3: E ::= ε
  E.trans_out = AllButFirst(E.trans_in);
  E.trans = if FIRST(E.trans_in) = 'b' then 'b'
    else ε;

p_4: $S_0 ::= S_1$ a
  S_0.value = Concatenate(S_1.value, S_1.value);
  S_1.trans_in = S_0.trans_in;
  S_0.trans_out = S_1.trans_out;
  S_0.trans = S_1.trans;

p_5: S ::= a
  S.value = 'bb';
  S.trans_out = AllButFirst(S.trans_in);
  S.trans = if FIRST(S.trans_in) = 'b' then 'b'
    else ε;

Figure 2-9: The AG of figure 2-8 converted to a RIF

The following corollary is a direct result of the theorem:

Corollary 2: Any translation described by an AG can be described by a RIF.

Let us reflect for a moment. Why is it that RIFs are as powerful as attribute grammars? Certainly this is due, at least in part, to the fact that a RIF does not restrict the way attributes other than the trans attribute is computed. But there are other reasons as well. For one, as used in the proof of the previous theorem, RIFs allow a whole tree deriving the empty string to have semantics attached to it. In appendix A it is shown that this capability truly adds to the computational power of RIFs. The appendix will present a restricted subset of RIFs which are useful in practice but which can be shown to define a strict subset of the translations defined by RIFs.

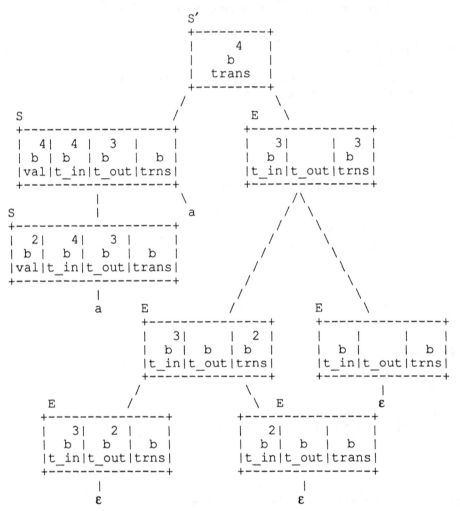

Figure 2-10: A typical semantic tree for the RIF of figure 2-9

This chapter has introduced RIFs and has compared them to syntax-directed translation schema and AGs. Our motivation for studying RIFs is presented in the next chapter, where we shall show that any RIF can be automatically inverted to form a specification of the inverse translation. The properties of inverted RIFs will also be examined.

Chapter 3

The inversion of RIF grammars

The basic premise of this thesis is that it is possible to generate a bi-directional translator from a one-way description of the translation. In this chapter we get to the "heart" of the matter by presenting the inversion algorithm for RIFs and proving its correctness. Section 3.1 contains the algorithm that, given an arbitrary RIF G, will produce the RIF G^{-1} specifying the inverse translation. Section 3.2 explores the properties of this generated inverse grammar. Most importantly, it is shown that the generated grammar actually specifies the inverse translation. In the last section the syntactic and semantic characteristics of the inverted RIF are examined.

3.1. The RIF inversion algorithm

In every RIF there exists a duality between the context-free portion of the production (the syntax of the production) and the semantic function defining the trans attribute of the left-part symbol X_0 (the semantics of the production). While the context-free portion defines the strings X_0 can legally derive, the semantic function computing X_0.trans defines the translation of such strings. The inversion process exploits this duality by switching the role of syntax and semantics.

Let Σ and Δ be finite alphabets and let G be a RIF specifying the translation T over $\Sigma \times \Delta$. The RIF G^{-1} specifying the inverse translation T^{-1} over $\Delta \times \Sigma$ is generated from G as follows:

1. For each symbol δ of Δ, create a terminal δ in G^{-1}.

2. For each nonterminal X in G, create a nonterminal XI in G^{-1} (we call it XI and not X to avoid confusion. We will not be very strict about this usage, however, when our meaning is clear. For example, when we refer to a semantic function f of G as also being a semantic function of G^{-1}, we mean

the semantic function f' that is obtained from f by substituting every occurrence of $X.A$ in f by $XI.A$).

3. Let each nonterminal XI in G^{-1} have the same set of attributes as X in G with one additional synthesized attribute, $XI.transinv$. The attribute transinv will play the same role in G^{-1} as the attribute trans did in G; i.e., the transinv attribute will take on values in $\Sigma^* \cup \{ \text{ERROR} \}$ and represents the translation of the substring that XI derives.

4. For each production $[p: X_0 ::= \alpha_0 X_1 \alpha_1 X_2 \dots X_{n_p} \alpha_{n_p}]$ in G with the distinguished semantic function

$X_0.\text{trans} =$
$\quad$ **if** $\text{ERROR}(X_1.\text{trans},\dots,X_{n_p}.\text{trans})$ **or** $g_1(\text{atts}_1)$

$\quad\quad\quad\quad$ **then ERROR**

$\quad$ **elsif** $g_2(\text{atts}_2)$ **then** $f_2(X_1.\text{trans},\dots,X_{n_p}.\text{trans})$

$\quad\quad\quad\quad \bullet$
$\quad\quad\quad\quad \bullet$
$\quad\quad\quad\quad \bullet$

$\quad$ **elsif** $g_{s-1}(\text{atts}_{s-1})$ **then** $f_{s-1}(X_1.\text{trans},\dots,X_{n_p}.\text{trans})$

$\quad$ **else** $f_s(X_1.\text{trans},\dots,X_{n_p}.\text{trans})$

create $s-1$ productions in G^{-1}, one corresponding to each of the token permuting functions f_j. In particular, for each f_j $(2 \le j \le s)$ where $f_j(X_1.\text{trans},\dots,X_{n_p}.\text{trans}) = \text{Concatenate}(\beta_0, X_{i_1}.\text{trans}, \beta_1, X_{i_2}.\text{trans},\dots, X_{i_{np}}.\text{trans}, \beta_{n_p})$ create an inverse production $[pI_j: XI_0 ::= \beta_0 XI_{i_1} \beta_1 XI_{i_2} \dots XI_{i_{np}} \beta_{n_p}]$. Let this production have all the semantic functions that p has except that in place of the semantic function defining $X_0.\text{trans}$ as given above, it has the semantic function $XI_0.\text{trans} = f_j(XI_1.\text{trans},\dots,XI_{n_p}.\text{trans})$. It also has one additional semantic function defining $XI_0.\text{transinv}$ given by

$XI_0.\text{transinv} =$
$\quad$ **if** $\text{ERROR}(XI_1.\text{transinv},\dots,XI_{n_p}.\text{transinv})$ **or** $g_1(\text{atts}_1)$

$\quad\quad$ **or** $g_2(\text{atts}_2)$ **or** $\dots$ **or** $g_{j-1}(\text{atts}_{j-1})$

$\quad\quad$ **or** $\text{NOT}(g_j(\text{atts}_j))$ **then ERROR**

$\quad$ **else** $\text{Concatenate}(\alpha_0, XI_1.\text{transinv}, \alpha_1,$
$\quad\quad\quad XI_2.\text{transinv},\dots, XI_{n_p}.\text{transinv}, \alpha_{np})$.

5. The value of the translation is specified to be the value of the transinv attribute of the root ($SI.\text{transinv}$).

This algorithm creates the inverse grammar G^{-1} modularly from G, production by production. Each production in G gives rise to one or more productions in G^{-1}. The inverse grammar G^{-1} will translate strings of Δ^* into strings of Σ^*. Since the semantic function defining XI_0.transinv (given in point 4) is defined by a token permuting clause, the inverse grammar G^{-1} is also a RIF. Hence, <u>RIFs are closed under the inversion algorithm</u>[9].

To make point 4 of the above algorithm more concrete, figure 3-1 shows the inversion of production p_6 of the RIF presented in figure 2-5. This production is <u>split</u> into two productions in the inverse attribute grammar. Whereas the production p_6 of the original RIF specified that Op derived 'multiply' and had a translation of either '$*_r$' or '$*_i$' the inverse productions pI_{6a} and pI_{6b} specify that OpI derives either '$*_r$' or '$*_i$' and in either case has a translation of 'multiply'. OpI's derivation of '$*_r$' or '$*_i$' will result in ERROR if certain conditions are not satisfied.

pI_{6a}: **OpI ::= $*_r$.**
    OpI.trans = '$*_r$';
    OpI.transinv = if NOT(OpI.type = decimal_pt) then ERROR
          else 'multiply';
pI_{6b}: **OpI ::= $*_i$.**
    OpI.trans = '$*_i$';
    OpI.transinv = if (OpI.type = decimal_pt) then ERROR
          else 'multiply';

Figure 3-1: The inversion of p_6 of figure 2-5 splits into two productions

Using the inversion algorithm, all the attributes of a nonterminal in the original RIF remain with the corresponding nonterminal of the inverse RIF. They will be defined properly since all the semantic functions of a production remain in the inverse production as well. Even the trans attribute remains in the inverse attribute grammar because it is no worse than any other attribute; it may be directly or indirectly used in some condition $g_j(atts_j)$ thereby influencing the translation. After the inverse RIF has been generated, however, it may become apparent that some of the trans attributes are

---

[9]Contrast this to the *generalized syntax-directed schema* of [7]. This grammar based translation methodology is also defined as a restricted AG, but it is not closed under inversion.

unnecessary. At this point those useless attributes and their corresponding semantic functions can be 'weeded out' of the inverse specification.

Figure 3-2 presents the entire inverse RIF obtained by applying the inversion algorithm to the RIF of figure 2-5. Productions pI_{6a} and pI_{6b} have already been shown; pI_7 and pI_8 are omitted. An important fact concerning the inversion algorithm can be illustrated using this RIF G and its generated inverse G^{-1}. Consider the string '$(80,5.8,*_i)$'. This string is not in the domain the translation specified by G; the RIF G would not translate any input string to '$(80,5.8,*_i)$'. This string is, however, recognized by the underlying context-free grammar of G^{-1}. Nonetheless, the semantic tree in G^{-1} that recognizes this string translates it to ERROR. In general, the generated inverse RIF will have an underlying context-free grammar that "covers" its domain and those strings in the covering language but not in the domain of the translation will be translated to ERROR.

3.2. Properties of inverted RIFs

This section establishes the "correctness" of the inversion algorithm of the last section; it is shown that if G is a RIF defining the translation T and G^{-1} is the inverse RIF generated from G by the inversion algorithm, then for all w ≠ ERROR and x ≠ ERROR, (w,x) is in T if and only if (x,w) is in T^{-1}, where T^{-1} is the translation specified by G^{-1}. In this section some other relationships between T and T^{-1} will also be exhibited. For example, it will be shown that if T is 1-1 then T^{-1} is 1-1. However, if T is not uniquely invertible then T^{-1} will not be a function and if T is not a function then T^{-1} will not be uniquely invertible. For the rest of this chapter, G refers to an arbitrary RIF specifying the translation T over $\Sigma \times \Delta$ and G^{-1} refers to the RIF generated from G by the inversion algorithm. G^{-1} specifies a translation T^{-1} over $\Delta \times \Sigma$. We refer to any semantic tree of a RIF translating w to x as *valid* if w ≠ ERROR and x ≠ ERROR.

The following discussion will provide a method of constructing a valid semantic tree in G^{-1} given a valid semantic tree in G and vice versa. It will then be shown that these two semantic trees are intimately related to one another; if one tree translates w to x, the

pI_1: SI ::= (NumberI1 , NumberI2 , OpI).
    SI.trans = Concatenate('(', NumberI1.trans, ',',
           NumberI2.trans, ',', OpI.trans,')');
    OpI.type = If (NumberI1.type = decimal_pt) or
        (NumberI2.type = decimal_pt)
      then decimal_pt else int;
    SI.transinv = If (OpI.trans='+$_r$') or (OpI.trans='+$_i$') then ERROR
        else Concatenate(OpI.transinv, NumberI1.transinv, 'by',
           NumberI2.transinv);

pI_2: SI ::= (NumberI1 , NumberI2 , OpI).
    SI.trans = Concatenate('(', NumberI1.trans, ',',
          NumberI2.trans, ',', OpI.trans,')');
    OpI.type = If (NumberI1.type = decimal_pt) or
        (NumberI2.type = decimal_pt)
      then decimal_pt else int;
    SI.transinv = If (OpI.trans='*$_r$') or (OpI.trans='*$_i$') then ERROR
        else Concatenate(OpI.transinv, NumberI1.transinv, 'to',
          NumberI2.transinv);

pI_3: NumberI ::= IntegerI.
    NumberI.trans = Concatenate(IntegerI.trans);
    NumberI.type = int;
    NumberI.transinv = Concatenate(IntegerI.transinv);

pI_4: NumberI ::= Decimal_numI.
    NumberI.trans = Concatenate(Decimal_numI.trans);
    NumberI.type = decimal_pt;
    NumberI.transinv = Concatenate(Decimal_numI.transinv);

pI_{5a}: OpI ::= +$_r$.
    OpI.trans = '+$_r$';
    OpI.transinv = if NOT(OpI.type = decimal_pt) then ERROR else 'add';

pI_{5b}: OpI ::= +$_i$.
    OpI.trans = '+$_i$';
    OpI.transinv = if (Op.type = decimal_pt) then ERROR else 'add';

Figure 3-2: The inverse RIF generated from the RIF of figure 2-5

other will translate x to w. This will provide the necessary tools to show that G and G^{-1} are really inverses of one another.

The first step in constructing a semantic tree in G^{-1} from one in G, is to construct a production in G^{-1} from a production in G. Let $[p: X_0 ::= \alpha_0 X_1 \alpha_1 X_2 ... X_{n_p} \alpha_{n_p}]$ be a production of G with the distinguished semantic function $<X_0.trans = $ if ERROR(X_1.trans,..., X_{n_p}.trans) or g_1(atts) then ERROR elsif g_2(atts) then $f_2(X_1$.trans,..., X_{n_p}.trans) elsif ... elsif g_{s-1}(atts) then $f_{s-1}(X_1$.trans,..., X_{n_p}.trans) else $f_s(X_1$.trans,...,

X_{n_p}.trans)>. Then there will be s-1 inverse productions, $pI_2,...,pI_s$, in G^{-1} corresponding to each of the s-1 token permuting functions in the token permuting clause defining X_0.trans. Let h map productions of G and an integer to productions of G^{-1}, such that $h(p,j) = pI_j$ if $2 \leq j \leq s$ and is undefined otherwise. We extend h to be a mapping from valid semantic trees of G to valid semantic trees of G^{-1} as follows: Let ST be a valid semantic tree of G. h(ST) is the valid semantic tree of G^{-1} obtained from ST by performing the following steps:

1. At each nonterminal node N of ST labeled by a production p, replace the label p by the label h(p,j), where f_j is the token permuting function used to define the distinguished attribute N.trans; i.e., in the token permuting clause used to evaluate N.trans, $g_1(atts_1) = g_2(atts_2) = ... \ g_{j-1}(atts_{j-1}) =$ false and $g_j(atts_j) =$ true. We refer to a node N as N' after it has been relabeled.

2. When relabeling a node N labeled p by pI_j, delete children who are terminals of Σ, add terminals of Δ, and permute the order of nonterminal node children as dictated by pI_j. For example, if p is of the form [A ::= a B C b] and pI_j is of the form [AI ::= CI q BI], then the order of B and C would be reversed, the terminals 'a' and 'b' would be deleted, and the terminal 'q' would be inserted between the subtrees rooted at C and B.

3. Add to each nonterminal node N' relabeled as pI_j the distinguished attribute N'.transinv and evaluate this attribute as dictated by the semantic function in pI_j.

Figure 3-3 gives a valid semantic tree ST for the RIF of figure 2-5 and figure 3-4 gives the inverse semantic tree obtained by applying the mapping h to ST.

The mapping h is certainly well-defined. The following lemmas will establish two other facts about the mapping h. Lemma 1 will show that the mapping produces valid semantic trees of G^{-1}. Lemma 2 will show that the mapping h is an isomorphism.

Lemma 1: Given a valid semantic tree ST of G, h(ST) is a valid semantic tree of G^{-1}.

Proof: To see that the output of h describes a semantic tree of G^{-1} (i.e., the context-free portion of the h(ST) describes a parse tree for the underlying context-free grammar G^{-1}), we show by induction that each node N' in h(ST) corresponding to the node N in ST will be the root of a legitimate subtree in G^{-1}. For the basis step, let N be a node of height 1. Then N is labeled by a production of the form [p: X ::= α], where α is in Σ^*.

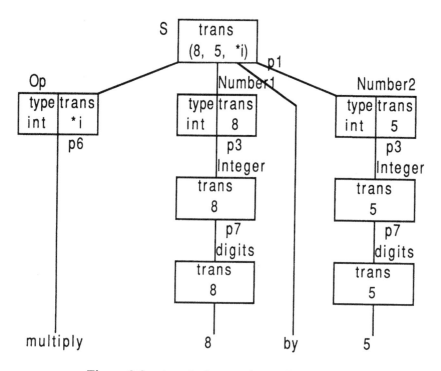

Figure 3-3: A typical semantic tree for the RIF of figure 2-5

The distinguished semantic function of p is of the form: $<X.\text{trans} = \text{if } g_1(...) \text{ then}$ ERROR elsif $g_2(...)$ then $f_2()$ elsif ... else $f_s()>$, where each $f_j()$ is a constant token permuting function returning some constant string in Δ^{*10}. Since the semantic tree is valid, one of these token permuting functions, say $f_j() = \beta \in \Delta^*$, is used to assign the value β to the attribute-instance N.trans. Therefore, in h(ST), N′ gets labeled by the production $[pI_j: XI ::= \beta]$ of G^{-1}. Hence N′ is the root of a legitimate subtree in G^{-1}. For the inductive step, assume that N is a node of ST of height h + 1 and is labeled by a production of the form $[p: X_0 ::= \alpha_0 X_1 \alpha_1 X_2 ... X_{n_p} \alpha_{n_p}]$. The distinguished semantic function of p is of the form: $<X_0.\text{trans} = \text{if ERROR}(X_1.\text{trans}, ..., X_{n_p}.\text{trans})$ or $g_1(...)$ then ERROR elsif $g_2(...)$ then $f_1(X_1.\text{trans}, ..., X_{n_p}.\text{trans})$ elsif ... else $f_s(X_1.\text{trans}, ..., X_{n_p}.\text{trans})>$, where each f_j is a token permuting function over Δ^*. Since the semantic tree is valid, one of these token permuting functions, say $f_j() = \text{Concatenate}(\beta_0, X_{i_1}.\text{trans}, \beta_1, X_{i_2}.\text{trans}, ..., X_{i_{np}}.\text{trans}, \beta_{n_p})$ is used to assign the value $\text{Concatenate}(\beta_0, N_{i_1}.\text{trans}, \beta_1,$

---

[10]It is a <u>constant</u> token permuting function because there are no right-part symbols in the production.

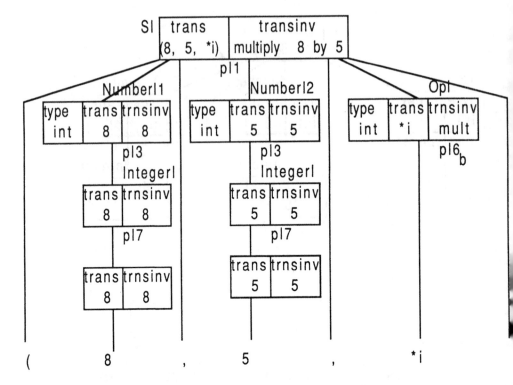

Figure 3-4: The inverse of the previous semantic tree

$N_{i_2}.trans, ..., N_{i_{np}}.trans, \beta_{np})$ to the attribute-instance N.trans, where N_i $(1 \leq i \leq n)$ is the ith child of N corresponding to X_i and each β_i is in Δ^*. Let $N', N_1', ..., N_{n_p}'$ be the nodes in h(ST) corresponding to the nodes $N, N_1, ..., N_{n_p}$ in ST. N' gets labeled by the production $[pI_j: XI_0 ::= \beta_0 XI_{i_1} \beta_1 XI_{i_2} ... XI_{i_{np}} \beta_{n_p}]$, $N_1', ..., N_{n_p}'$ get permuted into the order $N_{i_1}', ..., N_{i_{np}}'$, the α_i terminals attached to N get deleted, and the β_i terminals are inserted as children of N' in the appropriate places. Since $N_{i_1}', ..., N_{i_{np}}'$ are of height $\leq h$, they are, by induction, legitimate subtrees in G^{-1}. Therefore N' will be a legitimate subtree in G^{-1}. Hence if N is a node of ST, the corresponding node N' in ST' is the root of a legitimate subtree in ST'. We can therefore conclude that the root of h(ST), which corresponds to the root of ST, will be a legitimate subtree of G^{-1}. And since the root of ST is labeled by S, the goal symbol of G, the root of h(ST) will be labeled by SI, the goal symbol of G^{-1}. Hence h(ST) will be a semantic tree of G^{-1}.

To see that h(ST) is a <u>valid</u> semantic tree of G^{-1}, we must show that for every node N'

in ST, N'.transinv $\neq$ ERROR. This can be established by recalling that the semantic function defining N'.transinv is of the form: $<$if ERROR(XI_1.transinv,...,XI_{n_p}.transinv) or g_1(...) or ... g_{j-1}(...) or NOT(g_j(...)) then ERROR else ...$>$, where N' is labeled by pI_j. Since N.trans of the original semantic tree ST was not equal to ERROR, it must be that g_1(...) = false and since N' received the label pI_j, it must be that g_2(...) = ... = g_{j-1}(...) = false and g_j(...) = true (by point 1 in the definition of h)[11]. Since we can furthermore establish, by induction, that N_1'.transinv, ..., N_{n_p}'.transinv are not equal to ERROR, we conclude that N'.transinv will not equal ERROR. This establishes our claim that h(ST) is a valid semantic tree of G^{-1}. **End of proof.**

Lemma 2: h is an isomorphism.

Proof: Let h^{-1} define a mapping from trees in G^{-1} to trees in G by "reversing" the steps given in the mapping h; i.e., given a semantic tree ST' in G^{-1}, h^{-1} relabels each node labeled pI_j with p, deletes terminals in Δ and adds terminals in Σ, "unpermutes" the order of nonterminal nodes, and removes the transinv attribute. It is not hard to see that given any valid semantic tree ST' in G^{-1}, $h^{-1}(ST')$ will be a valid semantic tree in G. Furthermore, it can be shown that $h \circ h^{-1}$ is the identity function. Hence h is an isomorphism[12]. **End of proof.**

---

[11]This statement makes use of the fact that each attribute N'.att that is also an attribute of N (i.e., all attributes other than the transinv attribute) have the same value. This is because the semantic trees are isomorphic and the attributes are computed by the same semantic functions.

[12]That h is an isomorphism is dependent upon the fact that nodes are labeled by production numbers, and that two trees are equivalent only if the node labels are the same. Consider, for instance, the following RIF:

```
p1: A ::= B1 B2.
      A.trans = if (B1.num = 2) then Concat(B1.trans, B2.trans)
                  else Concat(B2.trans, B1.trans);
p2: B ::= c d.
      B.num = 2;
      B.trans = w x.
p3: B ::= e f.
      B.num = 3;
      B.trans = y z.
```

Both strings 'c d e f' and 'e f c d' translate to 'w x y z'. Let ST1 and ST2 be the semantic trees for 'c d e f' and 'e f c d' respectively. Then h(ST1) and h(ST2) have the same underlying parse tree, but they differ in the label associated with the root node. Whereas h(ST1) is labeled $pI1_1$, h(ST2) is labeled by $pI1_2$.

Lemma 2 declares that there exists an isomorphism (h) between valid trees in G and valid trees in G^{-1}. The nature of h is such that there exists a 1-1 mapping between interior nodes of ST and those of h(ST).

The next lemma shows that ST and h(ST) are intrinsically related to one another. In particular, h(ST) is the "inverse" of the semantic tree ST; if ST translates w to x, then h(ST) translates x to w. First we introduce the following notation: Let ST be a semantic tree of a RIF. For any node N of ST, $DERIV(N)$ is the terminal string that N derives and $VALUE(N)$ is the value of N's distinguished attribute (if the RIF has been automatically generated by the inversion algorithm then $VALUE(N) = $ N.transinv, otherwise $VALUE(N) = $ N.trans). We extend these definitions to semantic trees by defining $DERIV(ST) = DERIV(S)$ and $VALUE(ST) = VALUE(S)$, where S is the root node of the semantic tree ST.

Lemma 3: Given any valid semantic tree ST for the RIF G, $DERIV(ST) = VALUE(h(ST))$ and $VALUE(ST) = DERIV(h(ST))$.

Proof: Once again, we refer to N as a node in ST and to N′ as its corresponding node in h(ST). We will show by induction that for any nonterminal node N in ST, $DERIV(N) = VALUE(N')$ and $VALUE(N) = DERIV(N')$. The lemma follows from this fact. The induction proceeds on the height of the node in the tree.

Basis: Let N be a node of ST of height 1, labeled by the production [p: X ::= α], where α is in Σ^*. The distinguished semantic function of p is of the form: $<X_0.\text{trans} = \text{if } g_1(...)$ then ERROR elsif $g_2(...)$ then $f_2()$ elsif ... else $f_s()>$, where each $f_j()$ is a constant token permuting function returning some constant string in Δ^*. Since the semantic tree is valid, one of these token permuting functions, say $f_j() = \beta \in \Delta^*$, is used to assign the value β to the attribute-instance N.trans. Therefore $DERIV(N) = \alpha$ and $VALUE(N) = \beta$. By the definition of h, N′ will be labeled by the production [pI_j: XI ::= β]. The distinguished semantic function of pI has the form: $<XI.\text{transinv} = \text{if } g_1(...) \text{ or } g_2(...) \text{ or }$ ... or $g_{j-1}(...)$ or $NOT(g_j(...)))$ then ERROR else α>. Since h(ST) is valid, the attribute-instance N′.transinv will be assigned the value α. Hence $DERIV(N') = \beta = VALUE(N)$ and $VALUE(N') = \alpha = DERIV(N)$.

<u>Inductive step:</u> Let N be node of ST of height h + 1, labeled by the production [p: $X_0 ::= \alpha_0 X_1 \alpha_1 ... X_n \ \alpha_n$], where each α_i is in Σ^*. The distinguished semantic function of p is of the form: $<X.trans = $ if $ERROR(X_1.trans, ..., X_n.trans)$ or $g_1(...)$ then ERROR elsif $g_2(...)$ then $f_1(X_1.trans, ..., X_n.trans)$ elsif ... else $f_s(X_1.trans, ..., X_n.trans)>$, where each f_j is a token permuting function over Δ^*. Since the semantic tree is valid, one of these token permuting functions, say $f_j() = $ Concatenate$(\beta_0, X_{i_1}.trans, \beta_1, X_{i_2}.trans, ..., X_{i_n}.trans, \beta_n)$ is used to assign the value Concatenate$(\beta_0, N_{i_1}.trans, \beta_1, N_{i_2}.trans, ..., N_{i_n}.trans, \beta_n)$ to the attribute-instance N.trans, where N_i ($1 \le i \le n$) is the ith child of N corresponding to X_i and each β_i is in Δ^*. Therefore $DERIV(N) = $ Concatenate$(\alpha_0, Deriv(N_1), \alpha_1, DERIV(N_2), ..., DERIV(N_n), \alpha_n)$ and $VALUE(N) = $ Concatenate$(\beta_0, VALUE(N_{i_1}), \beta_1, VALUE(N_{i_2}), ..., VALUE(N_{i_n}), \beta_n)$. By the definition of h, N′ will be rooted at the production [pI_j: $XI_0 ::= \beta_0 XI_{i_1} \beta_1 XI_{i_2} ... XI_{i_n} \beta_n$] having the distinguished semantic function $<XI_0.transinv = $ if $ERROR(XI_1.transinv, ..., XI_n.transinv)$ or $g_1(...)$ or $g_2(...)$ or ... or $g_{j-1}(...)$ or $NOT(g_j(...))$) then ERROR else Concatenate$(\alpha_0, XI_1.transinv, \alpha_1, XI_2.transinv, ..., XI_n.transinv, \alpha_n).>$ Since h(ST) is valid, $DERIV(N′) = $ Concatenate$(\beta_0, DERIV(N_{i_1}′), \beta_1, DERIV(N_{i_2}′), ..., DERIV(N_{i_n}′), \beta_n)$ and $VALUE(N′) = $ Concatenate$(\alpha_0, VALUE(N_1′), \alpha_1, VALUE(N_2′), ..., VALUE(N_n′), \alpha_n)$. Since each N_i has height $\le$ h, by induction, $DERIV(N_i) = VALUE(N_i′)$ and $VALUE(N_i) = DERIV(N_i′)$ ($1 \le i \le n$). Hence $DERIV(N) = VALUE(N′)$ and $VALUE(N) = DERIV(N′)$. **End of proof.**

Using this lemma, we can establish the <u>fundamental theorem of inversion</u> which declares that the inversion algorithm is correct and produces the intended result.

Theorem 4: Let G be a RIF specifying the translation T. Let G^{-1} be the RIF generated from G by the inversion algorithm specifying the translation T^{-1}. Then, for all w ≠ ERROR and x ≠ ERROR, (w,x) is in T if and only if (x,w) is in T^{-1}.

Proof: If (w,x) is in T then there exists a valid semantic tree ST in G translating w to x. By lemma 1, h(ST) is a valid semantic tree in G^{-1} and, by lemma 3, h(ST) translates x to w. Hence (x,w) is in T^{-1}.

Similarly, if (x,w) is in T^{-1}, then there exists a semantic tree ST′ in G^{-1} translating x to w. Since h is an isomorphism (lemma 2), there exists a valid semantic tree in G such that h(ST) = ST′. By the previous lemma, ST translates w to x. Hence (w,x) is in T. **End of proof.**

Theorem 5: Given any attribute grammar specifying a translation T, there exists an algorithm to construct an inverse attribute grammar specifying the inverse translation T^{-1} such that for all w ≠ ERROR and x ≠ ERROR, (w,x) is in T if and only if (x,w) is in T^{-1}.

Proof: The specified algorithm is simply the composition of the algorithm given in section 2.2 converting an arbitrary attribute grammar to a RIF with the RIF inversion algorithm of the previous section. The theorem follows from theorems 1 and 4. **End of proof.**

The next corollary compares the relationship between the translations T and T^{-1}.

Corollary 6: Let T and T^{-1} be as in theorem 4. T is uniquely invertible if and only if T^{-1} is a function and T is a function if and only if T^{-1} is uniquely invertible.

Proof: Let T be uniquely invertible and let (w,x) and (w,x′) be in T^{-1} (w ≠ ERROR, x ≠ ERROR). By theorem 4, (x,w) and (x′,w) are in T. Since T is uniquely invertible x = x′. Hence T^{-1} is a function. Similarly, let T^{-1} be a function. If (x,w) and (x′,w) are in T, then (w,x) and (w,x′) are in T^{-1}. But since T^{-1} is a function x = x′ and therefore T is uniquely invertible. A similar proof establishes that T is a function if and only if T^{-1} is uniquely invertible. **End of proof.**

3.3. Syntactic and semantic evaluability of inverted RIFs

Although theorem 4 guarantees that the generated inverse grammar G^{-1} will be correct, it does not guarantee how efficient it will be. There are many criteria by which to judge the efficiency of a RIF. Two important criteria are syntactic and semantic efficiency. By asking how syntactically efficient is an AG, we mean how hard is it to recognize whether or not a string belongs to the language generated by the AG's underlying context-free grammar. Formal language theory provides a well-known hierarchy of context-free languages in which some classes of languages can be parsed more efficiently than others. For instance SLR(k) languages and LR(k) languages can be parsed more efficiently for small values of k than larger values, and LR(k) languages can be parsed more efficiently than ambiguous ones.

Similarly, when we ask how semantically efficient is an AG, we mean how hard is it to fill in all the attribute values of a semantic tree. Recent research on AGs has developed a hierarchical classification of AGs in which efficient evaluators can be built for some AGs and not for others. For example, some AGs can be evaluated in a single left-to-right pass. Other important classes of AGs that have been discussed in the literature are alternating-pass [31], absolutely non-circular [42], ordered [37], and uniform [60].

Our analysis of the syntactic and semantic efficiency of the inverse RIF will involve the following question: assuming that the original RIF belongs to a certain syntactic (semantic) class, will the inverse RIF also belong to that class? Let us first ask this question concerning syntax. We would ideally like to have a result stating that if the RIF G is SLR(k), LALR(K), LR(k), or unambiguous[13], then so is G^{-1}. Unfortunately, this is not the case. Rather, it turns out that there is very little we can say concerning the syntax of G^{-1} based on G. Even if G is LR(0), G^{-1} may be terribly ambiguous. This is because the syntax of G^{-1} is related to the token permuting functions of the semantics of G, which bears no correspondence to the context-free rules of G.

Actually, if G^{-1} is to be the true inverse of G, then it often <u>must</u> be ambiguous. For if G specifies a translation T which is not uniquely invertible (i.e., there exist two inputs w and w′, both translating to x), then T^{-1} will not be a function and G^{-1} will be ambiguous (there will be two semantic trees for input x in G^{-1}, one translating x to w and one to w′). However, even if G is unambiguous and T^{-1} is 1-1, the underlying context-free grammar

---

[13]When we say that an AG G is SLR(k), etc., we mean that its underlying context-free grammar is SLR(k).

of G^{-1} may be ambiguous. In particular, there may be two semantic trees for an input x, only one of which is valid. This is the case with the inverse grammar G^{-1} given in figure 3-2. Although G is unambiguous and T^{-1} is 1-1, on any input, both productions pI_1 and pI_2 could be applied. Only one will complete the tree into a <u>valid</u> semantic tree however. Which one is valid depends upon whether the input string specifies addition or multiplication. We summarize our discussion with the following theorem:

Theorem 7: Let G be a RIF and G^{-1} its generated inverse specifying the translation T^{-1}. G^{-1} may be ambiguous even if G is unambiguous and T^{-1} is 1-1.

The problem of syntactic ambiguity turns out to be very important when using AG inversion for source-to-source translations. This is due to the fact that source-to-source translations are often many-to-one. For this reason we will return to this issue in sections 5.3 and 7.1.

Now let us turn to the question of semantic efficiency. Our intuition tells us that, unlike the syntax of G and G^{-1}, the semantics of G and G^{-1} are strongly related. This is because an inverted production pI directly inherits the semantics of its corresponding production p, with one added semantic function per production (used to compute the transinv attribute). A formal analysis proves our intuition to be correct - for the most part. The following discussion shows that even if G is evaluable in alternating passes, G^{-1} may not evaluable by this method. Similarly, G^{-1} may not be ordered even if G is ordered. However, if G is absolutely non-circular (ANC) or uniform, then G^{-1} will also belong into these classes.

The following discussion assumes that the reader is familiar with the classes ALT (evaluable in alternating passes) [31], ORD (ordered) [37], ANC (absolutely non-circular) [42], and uniform [60]. For a survey of these and other methods see [64].

Theorem 8: The generated inverse G^{-1} may not belong to ALT even if G does.

Proof: The theorem is proved by way of an example. Let [p: X0 ::= X1 Y X2] be a production of G and let the symbols X and Y have attributes i (an inherited attribute), s (a synthesized attribute), and trans (the distinguished attribute). Let the dependencies for this production be as given in figure 3-5, where the solid arcs denote semantic function dependencies and the dotted arcs denote *transitive closure* (indirect) dependencies. Let the distinguished function of this production be <X0.trans = Concatenate(X1.trans, X2.trans, Y.trans)>. The inverted production pI is also given in figure 3-5.

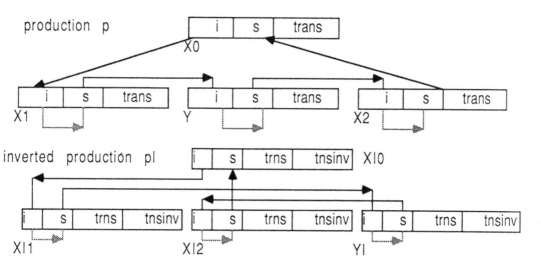

Figure 3-5: A production whose inverse is not evaluable in passes

In this case the attributes in production p are evaluable in a single left-to-right pass over the semantic tree. However, there is no assignment of pass numbers to the attributes of pI that will make it evaluable in alternating passes. This is because XI1.i must be evaluated before YI.i which must be evaluated before XI2.i. But there is no pass direction, either right-to-left or left-to-right, that would allow both XI1.i and XI2.i to be evaluated on the same pass. **End of proof.**

The reason why the inverse RIF may not be in ALT is because the inversion algorithm rearranges the order of the nonterminals in the production. Although all dependencies in the inverted production pI are the same as in the original production p, since the order of the nonterminals is different, the grammar may fail to be in ALT. For more powerful strategies the order of the nonterminals within the production is irrelevant. Although the order of nonterminals is irrelevant for ordered AGs, an inverted AG may fail to be ordered for another reason, even if the original AG is ordered. This is because the ordering algorithm introduces extra semantic dependencies to the attributes of a symbol in order to obtain a total order. Due to the way these edges are added, the original and inverse AGs may have different edges added causing one to be ordered and the other not to be.

Theorem 9: The generated inverse G^{-1} may not be ordered even if G is ordered.

Proof: The theorem is proved by way of an example, given in figure 3-6. Let [p: X ::= Y1 Y2] and [q: Y ::= w] be productions of G and let the distinguished semantic function of q be of the form: $<Y.trans = if\ g_1(Y.c)$ then ERROR else v>. The ordering strategy computes a total order on the attributes of each nonterminal symbol. If the total order introduces any cycles in the augmented dependency graphs then the grammar is not ordered, otherwise it is ordered. To obtain a total order, the strategy first adds any edges between attributes of the same symbol that are found in the dependency graphs. It then computes transitive closure (indirect) edges and adds them to the attributes of the symbols. If this does not induce a total ordering on the attributes of each symbol, another step is performed (called the DS relation by Kastens [37]) which adds extra dependencies to form a total order. In our example, the direct and indirect dependencies (given by solid and dotted lines) are enough to completely dictate the total order: (Y.a < Y.b < Y.c < Y.trans < Y.d < Y.e < Y.f < Y.g). This determines the *protocol* { {Y.a}, {Y.b}, {Y.c}, {Y.trans}, {Y.d}, {Y.e}, {Y.f}, {Y.g} } for the symbol Y; i.e., for every instance of Y in any semantic tree, the attribute-instance of Y.a will be evaluated before the attribute-instance of Y.b, and so forth. This AG is ordered since the DS relation does not introduce any cycles into the augmented dependency graphs.

When these productions are inverted, two important changes occur in the semantic functions. First of all, in place of the semantic function $<Y.trans = if\ g_1(Y.c)$ then ERROR else v>, the production qI contains the semantic function $<YI.trans = v>$.

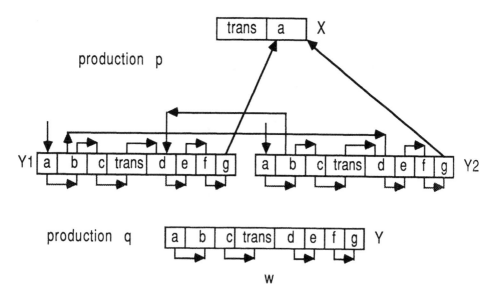

Figure 3-6: An ordered AG

Secondly, a new semantic function <YI.transinv = if g_1(Y.c) then ERROR else w> is added. The former change makes an important difference in the computation of the dependencies. Since YI.c no longer contributes to the semantic function computing YI.trans, in place of the total order: (Y.a < Y.b < Y.c < Y.trans < Y.d < Y.e < Y.f < Y.g) that existed in the original grammar, the inverted grammar only has a partial order given by: (YI.a < YI.b < YI.c < YI.transinv) and (YI.trans < YI.d < YI.e < YI.f < YI.g). This means that in order to obtain a total order, DS edges must be added. Among others, the edge (YI.d, YI.b) is added and the protocol { {YI.trans}, {YI.a, YI.d}, {YI.b, YI.e}, {YI.c, YI.f}, {YI.transinv, YI.g} } is produced for symbol YI. But this causes a cycle in the augmented dependency graph for pI. This can be seen by looking at figure 3-6, deleting the edges (Y1.c, Y1.trans) and (Y2.c, Y2.trans), and adding the edges (Y1.d, Y1.b) and (Y2.d, Y2.b). This causes the cycle: (Y1.b < Y2.d < Y2.b < Y1.d < Y1.b) in the augmented dependency graph for pI, and hence the inverted AG is not ordered. **End of proof.**

An inverted AG contains a subset of the semantic dependencies found in the original AG, except for dependencies relating to the introduced attribute transinv. The reason that the inverted may not be ordered even though the original AG is ordered is because the ordering algorithm introduces extra semantic dependencies. This enables it to establish a total order on the attributes of a symbol. Due to an idiosyncrasy of the inversion algorithm - namely, the fact that some dependencies are removed by the inversion algorithm- it turns out that the dependencies induced by the ordering algorithm on the inverted AG can be different than the dependencies induced on the original AG. If we consider a method that is less arbitrary in the edges it introduces then this problem will not arise. This is the case with ANC and uniform AGs.

Theorem 10: If G is in ANC [Uniform], G^{-1} will be in ANC [Uniform].

Proof: A formal proof is based upon the fact that, disregarding the transinv attribute, the extended dependency graphs for a production pI will contain a subset of the arcs found in the extended dependency graph for p. Since the only arcs involving transinv attributes will be from rignt-part symbol transinv attributes to the transinv attribute of the left-part symbol, these additional arcs will not cause any circularities in the extended dependency graph. Hence the inverted grammar will be ANC.

If the original grammar is uniform, then there will exist protocols for each nonterminal such that the protocols are consistent with the augmented dependency graphs. These same protocols can be used for the inverted nonterminals, with the slight modification of including the transinv attribute at the end of the protocol. Since (i) the protocols are consistent for the original grammar, (ii) each production pI_j contains a subset of the arcs found in the original production except for arcs leading into the transinv attribute of the left-part symbol, and (iii) transinv symbols only define other transinv symbols, these protocols will be consistent for the inverted grammar as well. Hence the inverse grammar will also be uniform. The details of these proofs are left to the reader (see also propositions 4 and 5 of [25] for similar constructions). **End of proof.**

In summary, most attribute evaluation strategies are guaranteed to work on G^{-1} if they work on G. However, the alternating-pass strategy is an exception to this rule. Nonetheless, in practice I found little problem in using the alternating-pass strategy on inverted RIFs. My source-to-source translators, described in chapter 6, used inverted

RIFs and produced alternating-pass evaluators. Only once did I encounter a RIF which inverted to a non-pass-evaluable AG. In this case, by slightly rewriting the original RIF, the problem was rectified.

In this chapter we have presented the inversion algorithm, and proved its correctness. We have also analyzed properties of inverted RIFs. In the next chapter show how to generalize RIFs and the inversion paradigm by allowing nonterminals to possess more than one trans attribute. Chapter 5 will then discuss INVERT, an AG inverter based upon the principles discussed in this and the next chapter.

Chapter 4

Generalizing RIFs

This chapter introduces a generalization of RIF grammars, which allows each nonterminal to contain several trans attributes instead of a single one. Before doing so, we need to ask ourselves why any generalization to RIFs is useful - we have already seen (theorems 1 and 4) that RIFs are capable of performing any translation. Since we cannot hope to gain any more expressive power, what is gained by generalizing RIFs?

The answer to this question is twofold. Firstly, although RIFs can theoretically express any translation, it is not always apparent how to do so. RIFs are very easy to write when the translations to be performed are similar to syntax-directed translation schema, bubbling the translation up the tree, requiring more power than syntax-directed translation schema only in order to control the manner in which permutations occur. However, when the translation needs to "duplicate", "split", or "delete" portions of translations in the semantic tree, it becomes much more difficult to express the translation by way of a RIF. This is because RIFs enforce a tree structure for a translation such that the inverse translation will have an isomorphic tree structure[14]. When the inverse translation is best expressed by a non-isomorphic structure, RIFs become difficult to write. Using multiple trans attributes is a natural and convenient way to express many sorts of translations.

An example, given in figure 4-1, illustrates this idea. The AG presented in this figure performs the translation $T((abc)^i) = a^i b^i c^i$ $(i \geq 1)$. Notice that it uses three trans

---

[14]See the commentary immediately following lemma 2 in chapter 3, where it is pointed out that for any valid semantic tree ST, there exists a valid inverse semantic tree ST' such that there is a 1-1 correspondence between the interior nodes of ST and ST'.

p_1: S ::= Y.
  S.trans = concat(Y.trans1, Y.trans2, Y.trans3);

p_2: Y_0 ::= a b c Y_1.
  Y_0.trans1 = concat('a', Y_1.trans1);
  Y_0.trans2 = concat('b', Y_1.trans2);
  Y_0.trans3 = concat('c', Y_1.trans3);

p_3: Y_0 ::= a b c.
  Y_0.trans1 = 'a';
  Y_0.trans2 = 'b';
  Y_0.trans3 = 'c';

----

p_1: S ::= Y1 Y2 Y3.
  S.trans = if NOT(length(Y1.trans) = length(Y2.trans) = length(Y3.trans))
      then ERROR
      else Y1.trans;

p_{2a}: $Y1_0$ ::= a $Y1_1$.
  $Y1_0$.trans = concat('abc', $Y1_1$.trans);

p_{2b}: $Y2_0$ ::= b $Y2_1$.
  $Y2_0$.trans = concat('abc', $Y2_1$.trans);

p_{2c}: $Y3_0$ ::= c $Y3_1$.
  $Y3_0$.trans = concat('abc', $Y3_1$.trans);

p_{3a}: Y1 ::= a.
  Y1.trans = 'abc';

p_{3b}: Y2 ::= b.
  Y2.trans = 'abc';

p_{3c}: Y3 ::= c.
  Y3.trans = 'abc';

Figure 4-1: An AG and its inverse

attributes. An inverse AG for this translation is also presented in the figure. Trying to
write these two translations as a RIF is very difficult, although, of course, it can be done.
This is because the natural way of writing the translation T and its inverse T^{-1}, as given
in figure 4-1, will result in non-isomorphic trees for a string s and its counterpart T(s).
Generalized RIFs described in this chapter will provide a method for writing AGs with
multiple trans attributes which still invert "nicely".

The second motivation for generalizing RIFs is for efficiency reasons. Even when it is apparent how to express a complicated translation with a RIF, it may not be an <u>efficient</u> way of expressing the translation. The inefficiency would take the form of ambiguity in the underlying context-free grammars of the original and inverse RIFs. For example, although the algorithm of chapter 2 transforms an arbitrary AG into an equivalent RIF, the generated RIF (and its inverse) would be terribly ambiguous. For any input string the RIF would specify many parse trees, only one of which would turn out to be semantically valid. Therefore, another goal in generalizing RIFs is to provide the RIF grammar writer with more machinery to express complicated translations that still invert "nicely"; i.e., without introducing unnecessary ambiguity into the inverse specification. The generalized RIFs of this chapter will allow one to express many translations unambiguously that would otherwise have to be specified by an ambiguous RIF. The subject of ambiguity will be dealt with more extensively in sections 5.3 and 7.1.

The remainder of this chapter defines *Generalized RIF Grammars* (GRIFs), gives the inversion algorithm for GRIFs, develops a system to evaluate inverted GRIFs, and proves the correctness of the inversion process. The reasons for generalizing RIFs, expressive power and efficiency, is supported intuitively by the examples of this chapter, as well as by our experience in writing and inverting RIFs. To support this claim on a more formal basis, one needs to formalize the concepts of expressive power and efficiency, and then compare GRIFs and RIFs based upon these criteria. For example, if we restrict RIFs and GRIFs to omit ε-productions, one can easily show that GRIFs surpass RIFs in expressive power. We leave such exercises to the reader.

4.1. GRIF grammars

In RIF grammars, each nonterminal has a single trans attribute and at each interior node of the parse tree, this attribute contains the translation of the subtree beneath it. If the translation of a subtree can best be viewed as two or more parts that are not to be consecutive in the output string, it is often difficult to express the translation as a RIF. GRIF grammars allow a nonterminal to have several trans attributes, thereby allowing them to express these sorts of translations quite easily. The inverse GRIF grammar will contain one nonterminal for each trans attribute of a symbol. Just as a RIF requires the distinguished left-part trans attribute to be defined by a token permuting clause involving right-part trans attributes, so too in a GRIF each left-part trans attribute must be defined by a token permuting clause involving right-part trans attributes. As in RIFs, these token permuting clauses will form the productions of the inverse grammar. The use of multiple trans attributes, however, complicates the inversion process.

If R is a RIF, R^{-1} its inverse, and T a tree in R translating s to m, then in R^{-1} there will exist a tree T^{-1} _isomorphic_ to T translating m to s. Once this isomorphic tree T^{-1} is discovered, it is easy to recover the string s since, in essence, we have the parse tree for s. In GRIFs, however, the process is not quite so simple. If T is a parse tree for a GRIF G, translating s to m, the inverse parse tree T^{-1} in G^{-1}, will not necessarily be isomorphic to T. In particular, a subtree of T may be duplicated several times in T^{-1}, or it may be split apart and reconstructed in T^{-1}, so that T^{-1} is no longer recognizable as an isomorphic image of T. Nonetheless, the formulation of GRIFs ensures that T^{-1} contains enough information to recover a tree isomorphic to T. This is done by a process called _tree unification._ This process can be viewed as a tree transformer: it would take the parse tree T^{-1} for m and create a new tree, T', isomorphic to T. Once this tree is obtained, it is an easy task to recover the translation s.

Figures 4-2 and 4-3 illustrate this idea. The first figure gives a semantic tree T for a GRIF using multiple trans attributes, and the next figure gives its inverse tree T^{-1}. Each trans attribute of T which contributes to the translation (contributes either directly or indirectly to S.trans) becomes a node of T^{-1}. So, for example, Y.trans1 and Y.trans2 become nodes Y1 and Y2 in T^{-1}, but X.trans3, Z.trans2, and W.trans2, because they don't contribute to the translation, do not have corresponding nodes in T^{-1}. The tree unification process would accept T^{-1} and by "unifying" nodes such as Y1 and Y2, create a tree isomorphic to the original one. This isomorphic tree would then yield the inverse translation.

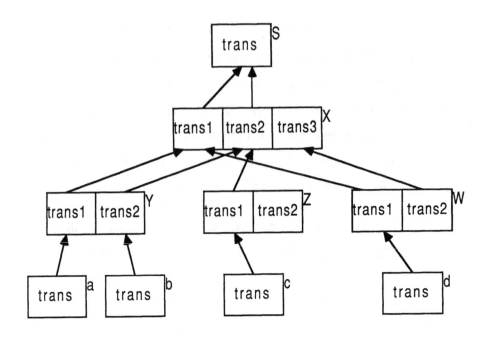

Figure 4-2: A semantic tree with multiple trans attributes

It is only possible to unify an inverse tree to an isomorphic representation of the original tree if sufficient information is present in the inverse tree. For example, if in figure 4-2 the attribute W.trans1 did not contribute to the translation, then there would be no corresponding node W1 in the inverse tree and therefore the tree unification process would not be able to recover the structure of the subtree rooted at W. The formulation of GRIFs must insure that enough trans attributes contribute to the translation in the original tree so that this situation does not arise. In the following sections these ideas will be made more precise.

4.1.1. A definition of GRIFs

In order to define GRIFs, it is useful to first define a generalized grammar based translation methodology, *multiple trans AGs*, which allows for multiple trans attributes. Multiple trans AGs combine the characteristics of Generalized SDTS and RIFs. Like Generalized SDTS, this grammar based translation methodology allows for multiple trans attributes. Like RIFs, it allows "semantic" attributes to play a role in the

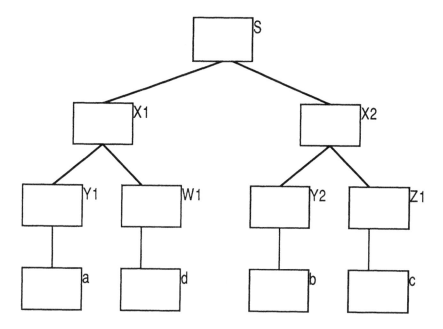

Figure 4-3: The inverse semantic tree

translation. (Generalized SDTS does not contain any "semantic" attributes, only "syntactic" ones). Both Generalized SDTS and RIFs are contained within the class of multiple trans AGs.

Let Σ and Δ be two finite alphabets. A *multiple trans attribute grammar* G defining the translation T over $\Sigma \times \Delta$, is an attribute grammar obeying the following restrictions:

1. Every nonterminal X of G has a set of distinguished synthesized attributes TRANS(X) = {X.trans1,...,X.transk} with k ≥ 1. Each trans attribute of TRANS(X) takes on values in $\Delta^* \cup$ { ERROR }.

2. TRANS(S), where S is the start symbol, consists of the singleton set {S.trans}. The value of the translation resides in the trans attribute of the root (S.trans).

3. For each production [p: $X_0 ::= \alpha_0 X_1 \alpha_1 X_2 \ldots X_{n_p} \alpha_{n_p}$], X_0.transA is defined by a **token permuting clause** of the form $h_A(X_{i_1}.transQ_1,...,X_{i_v}.transQ_v; atts_1, ..., atts_{s-1})$ where $1 \le i_j \le n_p$ for each j $(1 \le j \le v)$, and where each $atts_k$ $(1 \le k \le s-1)$ is a subset of $A(p)$. Note that the "string" arguments to each h_A must be trans attributes of the production's right-part nonterminals, but need not obey any other restrictions.

A multiple trans AG is a first approximation to GRIF grammars. Each nonterminal Y of a multiple trans AG will have one or more trans attributes, Y,trans1, ..., Y,transk. Each production $[p: X_0 ::= \alpha_0 \, X_1 \, \alpha_1 \, X_2 \, ... \, X_{n_p} \, \alpha_{n_p}]$ with $X_0 = Y$ will have a token permuting clause defining X_0.transA ($1 \leq A \leq k$). This function will be of the form:

X_0.transA =

   if $\mathbf{ERROR}(X_{i_1}.transQ_1,...,X_{i_v}.transQ_v)$ or $g_1(atts_1)$ then $\mathbf{ERROR}$

   elsif $g_2(atts_2)$ then $f_2(X_{i_1}.transQ_1, \, ...,X_{i_v}.transQ_v)$

   .
   .
   .

   elsif $g_{s-1}(atts_{s-1})$ then $f_{s-1}(X_{i_1}.transQ_1, \, ...,X_{i_v}.transQ_v)$

   else $f_s(X_{i_1}.transQ_1,...,X_{i_v}.transQ_v)$.

The function defining a trans attribute in a multiple trans AG is like the function defining a trans attribute in a RIF except that in a RIF, the "string" arguments to the token permuting clause are <u>exactly</u> the trans attributes of the right-part symbols of the production. In a multiple trans AG, however, some right-part symbols may not contribute any trans attributes whereas others may contribute several different trans attributes. Furthermore, a single trans attribute may appear several times as different string arguments.

In inverting a multiple trans AG, each trans attribute X.transA becomes an inverse nonterminal, XA. Each token permuting function defining X.transA becomes an inverse production with XA as its left-part symbol. For example, if [p: X ::= Y Z] is a production with the semantic function <X.trans1 = Concatenate(Y.trans1, Z.trans1, Y.trans2)>, then its corresponding inverse production would be $[p_1: X1 ::= Y1\ Z1\ Y2]$. The problem with this scheme occurs when not enough right-part trans attributes are involved. For example, if the semantic function defining X.trans1 was <X.trans1 = Concatenate(Y.trans1, Y.trans2)>, instead of the one given above, the inverse production would be $[p_1: X1 ::= Y1\ Y2]$. In this case there is no trace of Z in the inverse production. If the token permuting clauses defining other trans attributes of X similarly omitted trans attributes of Z, there would be no way for the tree unification process to reconstruct the subtree rooted at Z, given only the inverted tree.

In order to insure that every structure of the original tree is preserved in the inverse tree, multiple trans AGs need to be further restricted. One way to do this would be to require _every_ trans attribute to contribute to the translation. This is overly restrictive- it suffices to require that every node in the semantic tree contribute one trans attribute to the translation. In order to decide whether a multiple trans AG will fulfill this requirement, we define a partial order called COVER on TRANS(X).

Let G be a multiple trans AG and let C be a relation such that $C \subseteq \bigcup_{X \text{ is a nonterminal of } G} \{TRANS(X) \times TRANS(X)\}$. C satisfies the _cover condition_ if

for every $(X.transA, X.transB) \in C$

  for every production $[p: X_0 ::= \alpha_0 X_1 \alpha_1 X_2 \dots X_{n_p} \alpha_{n_p}]$ in G with $X = X_0$

    for any string argument $X_j.transF$ $(1 \leq j \leq n_p)$ of the token permuting clause defining $X_0.transB$ in p

      there exists a string argument $X_j.transE$ of the token permuting clause defining $X_0.transA$ in p such that $(X_j.transE, X_j.transF) \in C$.

For a given G, there may be many different relations which satisfy the cover condition. For example, the relation $\varnothing$ always satisfies the cover condition. Let $C' = \{C \mid C$ satisfies the cover condition$\}$. Note that (i) C' is a finite set and (ii) $C_1, C_2 \in C'$ implies that $C_1 \cup C_2 \in C'$. Therefore it makes sense to talk about the maximal element of C' (using the ordering induced by set inclusion). For any GRIF G, $COVER_G$ is defined to be the maximal element of C'. When G is clear from the context, $COVER_G$ is simply written as COVER. The relation COVER is _transitive_.

Although $COVER_G$ is defined as a relation on the trans attributes of the grammar G, it also expresses a property concerning semantic trees of G. Let ST be a semantic tree of the multiple trans AG G, N1 a node of ST, and N2 a descendant of N1. We say that N2 _contributes_ to N1.transA if (i) N2 is the son of N1 and the token permuting clause defining N1.transA takes a trans attribute of N2 as a string argument or (ii) there exists a son N3 of N1, the semantic function defining N1.transA takes a trans attribute of N3, N3.transC, as a string argument, and N2 _contributes_ to N3.transC. Given a node N1 of a semantic tree of G, if any node N2 in N1's subtree that *contributes* to N1.transB also *contributes* to N1.transA, then we say that N1.transA *covers* N1.transB. Proposition 1 relates the COVER relation, defined on attributes of the grammar G, to trees of G. The proposition is only presented to help the reader understand the significance of the COVER relation; it will not be used subsequently. The proof is therefore omitted.

> **Proposition 1:** Let G be a multiple trans AG. Given a node N labeled X in a semantic tree of G, if X.transA $COVER_G$ X.transB then N.transA *covers* N.transB.

A set $T = \{X.transA_1,...,X.transA_n\} \subseteq TRANS(X)$ is called a *complete trans set* for a nonterminal X if for every X.transB $\in$ TRANS(X), there exists an attribute $X.transA_k \in$ T such that $X.transA_k$ COVER X.transB. A complete trans set for a nonterminal need not be unique, but it cannot be empty. If If T is a complete trans set for a nonterminal X, then for any node labeled X in any semantic tree for G, the attributes of T contain as much information concerning the structure of the subtree beneath X as is available from any other set of trans attributes. The boolean function completeTransSet of figure 4-4 takes a nonterminal X and a set $T \subseteq TRANS(X)$. It returns true if T is a complete trans set for X and false otherwise. The function makes use of the COVER relation, which must be computed once for any grammar

```
boolean completeTransSet(T: setOfTransAttributes, X: nonterminal);
begin
    if for every X.transB in TRANS(X)
        there exists X.transA in T such that X.transA COVER X.transB
    then return(true)
    else return(false)
end;
```

Figure 4-4: Verifying a complete trans set

Let $[p: X_0 ::= \alpha_0 X_1 \alpha_1 X_2 ... X_{n_p} \alpha_{n_p}]$ be any production of a multiple trans AG. $ARGS_p(k)$ $(1 \leq k \leq n_p)$ is the set of trans attributes of X_k that are string arguments to some token permuting clause defining a left-part trans attribute. With this background, the definition of GRIF grammars can finally be given:

Let Σ and Δ be two finite alphabets. A *GRIF (generalized RIF) grammar defining the translation T* over $\Sigma \times \Delta$ is a multiple trans attribute grammar such that, for any production [p: $X_0 ::= \alpha_0 X_1 \alpha_1 X_2 ... X_{n_p} \alpha_{n_p}$] of G, $ARGS_p(k)$ is a complete trans set for X_k.

By forcing each right-part nonterminal to have a complete set of trans attributes contributing to the left-part trans attributes, GRIFs ensure that, for any semantic tree, each node contributes at least one trans attribute to the translation. This fact follows from the following proposition, whose proof is omitted.

Proposition 2: Let G be a GRIF, N a node of a semantic tree of G labeled X, and $\{X.transA_1, ..., X.transA_r\}$ a complete trans set for X. Then every (nonterminal) node in N's subtree *contributes* to some N.transA $\in$ $\{N.transA_1, ..., N.transA_r\}$.

It follows from the proposition that every node of a semantic tree ST contributes to the trans attribute of the root of ST.

In a RIF grammar, if any trans attribute of a node evaluates to ERROR, the translation will be ERROR. This is not true in GRIF grammars, where not every trans attribute in the semantic tree necessarily contributes to the translation.

4.1.2. The inversion of GRIFs

The inversion of a GRIF grammar will create two sets of productions. The first set will be context-free productions and will be used to parse input strings. The second will be called a *canonical* set of productions and will have associated semantic functions, as in regular AGs. Evaluating a string using the inverse GRIF will proceed in four stages: (i) parse the string using the context-free productions, (ii) "unify" the parse tree produced by stage i to create a "unified" semantic tree made up of canonical productions, (iii) evaluate the unified semantic tree using the associated semantic functions, and (iv) check the semantic tree for validity. The evaluation of strings using inverted GRIFs along with the tree unification algorithm is discussed in the next section; this section discusses how to create the inverse context-free and canonical productions from a given GRIF.

Formally, an inverted GRIF G^{-1} consists of a tuple (PRODS, SEM) where PRODS is the set of *parsing productions* and SEM is the *canonical set of productions*. Whereas PRODS = (N, Σ, S, P) is a context-free grammar, SEM is an AG, consisting of a set of productions and a set of semantic rules to evaluate the attributes associated with the productions. For purposes of symmetry, one can view the original GRIF G as also consisting of a tuple (PRODS, SEM). In this case, the context-free productions PRODS are the same as the productions of SEM, hence only trivial tree unification is needed. The parse tree is itself the unified semantic tree.

Let Σ and Δ be finite alphabets and let G be a GRIF grammar specifying the translation T over $\Sigma \times \Delta$. The inverse GRIF grammar G^{-1} = (PRODS, SEM) specifying the inverse translation T^{-1} over $\Delta \times \Sigma$ is generated from G in two steps. The first step generates the context-free grammar PRODS as follows:

1. For each symbol δ of Δ, create a terminal δ in PRODS.

2. For each nonterminal X in G such that TRANS(X) = {X.trans1, ..., X.transK}, create K nonterminals X1, ..., XK in PRODS. XA ($1 \leq A \leq K$) is said to be an *inverted X symbol*.

3. For each production [p: X_0 ::= α_0 X_1 α_1 X_2 ... X_{n_p} α_{n_p}] in G, let $h_A(X_{i_1}.transQ_1, ..., X_{i_v}.transQ_v$; $atts_1, ..., atts_{s-1}$) be the token permuting clause computing $X_0.transA$, where TRANS(X_0) = {$X_0.trans1$, ..., $X_0.transK$} and $1 \leq A \leq K$. Let h_A be of the form:

$X_0.transA =$
    if ERROR($X_{i_1}.transQ_1,...,X_{i_v}.transQ_v$) or $g_1(atts_1)$ then ERROR

    elsif $g_2(atts_2)$ then $f_2(X_{i_1}.transQ_1, ...,X_{i_v}.transQ_v)$

    .
    .

    elsif $g_{s-1}(atts_{s-1})$ then $f_{s-1}(X_{i_1}.transQ_1, ...,X_{i_v}.transQ_v)$

    else $f_s(X_{i_1}.transQ_1,...,X_{i_v}.transQ_v)$.

For each such token permuting clause h_A ($1 \leq A \leq K$), create s-1 <u>context-free</u> productions in PRODS, one corresponding to each of the token permuting functions f_t. In particular, for each f_t ($2 \leq t \leq s$) where
$f_t(X_{i_1}.transQ_1,...,X_{i_v}.transQ_v)$ =
Concatenate(β_0, $X_{i_{j1}}.transQ_{j1}$, β_1, $X_{i_{j2}}.transQ_{j2}$, ..., $X_{i_{jv}}.transQ_{jv}$, β_v)
computing $X_0.transA$, create an inverse context-free production

$[p_{A_t}: X_0 A ::= \beta_0 \ X_{i_{j_1}} Q_{j_1} \ \beta_1 \ X_{i_{j_2}} Q_{j_2} \ ... \ X_{i_{j_v}} Q_{j_v} \ \beta_v].$ (The subscripting here may be a little confusing. $X_{i_j} Q_j$ is the inverse symbol associated with $X_{i_j}.transQ_j$.) $X_{i_j} Q_j$ is said to be an *inverted* X_{i_j} *symbol of* p[15].

This creates the PROD part of G^{-1}. The SEM part is created as follows:

1. The set of nonterminals and terminals in SEM are the same as in G.

2. Each nonterminal of SEM will have all the attributes it had in G. In addition each nonterminal X will have a distinguished synthesized attribute X.transinv taking on values in Σ^*.

3. Each production $[p: X_0 ::= \alpha_0 \ X_1 \ \alpha_1 \ X_2 \ ... \ X_{n_p} \ \alpha_{n_p}]$ of G, is also in G^{-1}. It will have all of p's semantic functions and will, in addition, have a token permuting function of form: $X_0.transinv = Concatenate(\alpha_0, X_1.transinv, \alpha_1, X_2.transinv,..., X_{n_p}.transinv, \alpha_{n_p}).$

G^{-1} also has two mappings, CANONICAL and CONDITION, associated with it. CANONICAL maps every inverted production in PRODS to the production in SEM which gave rise to it: $CANONICAL(p_{A_t}) = p$. CONDITION associates a semantic condition to every production in PROD: $CONDITION(p_{A_t}) = not(g_1(...))$ and $not(g_2(...))$ and ... $not(g_{t-1}(...))$ and $g_t(...)$, where the g_j's ($1 \leq j \leq t$) are the first t conditions associated with the token permuting clause computing $X_0.transA$ in $CANONICAL(p_{A_t})$.

As an example, consider the GRIF grammar presented in the first part of figure 4-1. By running this GRIF through the inversion algorithm, the inverse GRIF of figure 4-5 will be produced. Note that the context-free productions of PRODS are similar to the productions of the inverse AG in figure 4-1. The productions of SEM, however, are similar to the productions of the original AG of that figure. In this example, $CONDITION(p_{A_t})$ will be empty (or, one could say, it will simply equal true) as there are no clauses g_t associated with any of the original productions.

---

[15] It is important to note that if the nonterminal $X_{i_j} Q_j$ of p_{A_t} is an inverted X_{i_j} symbol of p, it tells you not only that $X_{i_j} Q_j$ is an inverted X_{i_j} symbol, but it also tells you which occurrence of X_{i_j} in p gave rise to it. For example, if $[p: X ::= Y_1 \ Z \ Y_2]$ and $X.transA = Concatenate[Y_2.transA, Z.transA, Y_2.transB, Y_1.transB]$ then the inverted production corresponding to this token permuting function would be $[p_1: XA ::= YA \ ZA \ YB_1 \ YB_2]$. In this case YA is an inverted Y_2 symbol of p (which says more than just that YA is an inverted Y symbol), YB_1 is an inverted Y_2 symbol of p, and YB_2 is an inverted Y_1 symbol of p. In other words, in p_1, YB_1 corresponds to a trans attribute of the second occurrence of Y in p, whereas YB_2 corresponds to the first occurrence of Y in p.

The set of parsing productions PRODS:
p_1: S ::= Y1 Y2 Y3.

p_{2a}: $Y1_0$ ::= a $Y1_1$.

p_{2b}: $Y2_0$ ::= b $Y2_1$.

p_{2c}: $Y3_0$ ::= c $Y3_1$.

p_{3a}: Y1 ::= a.

p_{3b}: Y2 ::= b.

p_{3c}: Y3 ::= c.

The canonical set of productions SEM:
p_1: S ::= Y.
   S.trans = concat(Y.trans1, Y.trans2, Y.trans3);
   S.transinv = Y.transinv;

p_2: Y_0 ::= abc Y_1.
   Y_0.trans1 = concat('a', Y_1.trans1);
   Y_0.trans2 = concat('b', Y_1.trans2);
   Y_0.trans3 = concat('c', Y_1.trans3);
   Y_0.transinv = Concat('a', 'b', 'c', Y_1.transinv);

p_3: Y ::= abc.
   Y.trans1 = 'a';
   Y.trans2 = 'b';
   Y.trans3 = 'c';
   Y.transinv = Concat('a', 'b', 'c');

Figure 4-5:   An inverted GRIF

4.1.3. An evaluator for inverted GRIFs

As mentioned above, the evaluation process for inverted GRIFs now becomes slightly more complicated than in regular AGs or RIFs. The evaluation process will have the following stages:

   1. Parse the input string using the context-free grammar PRODS,

   2. unify the parse tree to produce a unified semantic tree in SEM,

   3. evaluate the semantic tree, and

   4. check for violated semantic conditions.

If each stage succeeds, the translation will be found in the distinguished transinv attribute of the root. If the evaluation fails in the first stage, i.e., a parse cannot be found for the input string, then the string must not be in domain of the translation. If it fails on any of the successive stages, then all that can be said for sure is that <u>this parse</u> for the string cannot produce a valid translation. Just as in RIFs, in order to be sure that there is no possible valid translation for this string, all parses must be tried.

Note that evaluation of semantic conditions is separate from the evaluation of the tree, unlike RIFs where the conditions are incorporated into the semantic evaluation process. This is because conditions are associated with productions in PRODS, not productions in SEM. During tree unification, when the parse tree is transformed into a semantic tree, information is recorded at each node of the tree concerning what conditions must be satisfied there. After evaluation of the semantic tree is complete, these conditions are checked to make sure that they have indeed been satisfied. With a little more effort this process could be incorporated into the semantic evaluation phase (see section 4.2, point 5), but for simplicity of presentation, the following discussion treats semantic condition evaluation as a separate phase.

Figures 4-6 and 4-7 give the tree unification algorithm. Each node N in a parse tree is assumed to have two fields: N.prod_label = p if the production p applies at that node and N.sym_label = X if X is the left-part symbol of p. (Of course the second label can be obtained from the first but using both labels simplifies the presentation). To unify a parse tree of the inverted GRIF G^{-1}, initially unifyTree(P, R′) is called, where P is the root node of the parse tree. If this procedure returns true, then the root of the unified tree is R′. The function unifyTree makes use of the recursive function unifyNodes. This function, in turn, makes use of three auxillary functions: completeTransSet (given in figure 4-4), equalTrees, and makeNode. The boolean function equalTrees is passed two nodes of a parse tree and returns the value true if the subtrees beneath these nodes are identical, otherwise it returns the value false. The procedure makeNode(p: prodType, N_1, ..., N_{n_p}: nodes, C: setOfSemanticConditions) takes a production label p, a (variable) number of nodes $N_1,...,N_{n_p}$ (the actual number depending upon p), and a set of semantic conditions. It returns a node (for the canonical semantic tree in SEM) labeled by the production $[p: X_0 ::= \alpha_0 X_1 \alpha_1 X_2 \dots X_{n_p} \alpha_{n_p}]$ with children $\alpha_0, N_1, \alpha_1, \dots, N_{n_p}, \alpha_{n_p}$, where α_i $(1 \leq i \leq n_p)$ are terminal nodes. In addition, this node will have a field containing the associated semantic conditions C, and any other necessary attribute fields which are associated with X_0 (the left-part symbol of p) in SEM.

The main part of the tree unification algorithm is found in the function UnifyNodes. This function takes a set Mlist of parse tree nodes and returns true if these nodes can be unified into a single node and their subtrees unified into a single subtree, whose structure is isomorphic to the original subtree[16]. The first step in this algorithm is to make sure that the nodes in Mlist can themselves be unified into a single node; i.e., that they represent trans attributes of a single node in the original tree. This is done by examining their labels. The next step considers whether or not the nodes in Mlist contain enough information to recover the original tree; i.e., whether or not these nodes correspond to a complete trans set in the original tree. At this point the function also makes sure that any nodes in Mlist corresponding to the same trans attribute in the original tree have identical subtrees. If the nodes in Mlist fail to meet these conditions the function returns false. Otherwise the function matches up the appropriate children of each node in Mlist and recursively calls itself on these sets of nodes. If all of the children can be successfully unified, then the function creates a new "unified" node having the appropriate "unified" children nodes, and returns true.

Let ST' be a semantic tree in SEM. ST' is said to be *valid* if the conditions associated with every node in ST' (by way of the tree unification algorithm) evaluate to true. ST' *evaluates to s* if R' is the root of ST' and R'.transinv = s.

The translation T^{-1} defined by an inverted GRIF $G^{-1} = $ (PRODS, SEM) are those pairs (m, s) such that
    1. there exists a parse tree for m in PRODS rooted at P,

---

[16]The term "original (sub)tree" used here refers to the tree of the the original GRIF performing the inverse translation. For example, if this semantic tree specifies the translation from m to s, then the original tree specifies the translation from s to m.

```
boolean unifyTree(P: parseTreeNode, R': SemNode);
begin
   return(unifyNodes({P}, R'));
end;
```

```
boolean function UnifyNodes(Mlist: setOfParseTreeNodes, N: SemNode);
```

/* This function is passed a set of nodes, Mlist. If it is successful in unifying these nodes it returns the value true and the unified node N. Otherwise it returns the value false. In order to unify these nodes, their corresponding children nodes must be unified. */

```
begin

   int j;

   prod_label p;

   setOfTransAttributes S;
```

/* maxRhs is a constant. For any production [p: $X_0 ::= \alpha_0 X_1 \alpha_1 X_2 ... X_{n_p} \alpha_{n_p}$], $n_p \leq$ maxRhs. */

```
   setOfParseTreeNodes T, Mlist_1, ..., Mlist_{maxRhs};

   SemNode N_1, ..., N_{maxRhs};

   conditions: setOfSemanticConditions;

   For any M in Mlist do
     p := CANONICAL(M.prod_label); /* [p: X_0 ::= \alpha_0 X_1 \alpha_1 X_2 ... X_{n_p} \alpha_{n_p}] */
```

/* All the nodes in Mlist must be labeled by inverted p productions. */

```
   For every M in Mlist do
     if CANONICAL(M.prod_label) ≠ p then return(false)
   endFor;

S := ∅; T := ∅;
```

Figure 4-6: The tree unification algorithm

```
/* The nodes in Mlist must comprise a complete trans set in order to recover
   the original semantic tree.  Furthermore, any two instances of the same
   nonterminal must have the same structure beneath them. */
For every M in Mlist do
   if M.sym_label = X₀A (for some inverted symbol X₀A of X₀)
        and X̄₀.transA is not already in S
   then
      begin
        add X₀.transA to S;
        add M to T
      end;
   else
      begin
        let M′ be the node already in T such that M′.sym_label= X₀A;
        if not(equalTrees(M′, M)) then return(false);
      end
endFor;
```

If not(completeTransSet(S, X₀)) then return(false);

```
/* The nodes in T must now be unified into a single node.  This requires
   recursively unifying the appropriate children nodes. */
For j := 1 to n_p
   Mlist_j := ∅;
   For each node M in T
      For each child M′ of M
        if M′.sym_label is an inverted X_j symbol of p
        then Mlist_j := Mlist_j ∪ {M′};
      endFor
   endfor;
   If Not(UnifyNode(Mlist_j, N_j)) then return(false);
endFor;
```

/* At this point all of the children have been successfully unified into nodes
   N_j ($1 \leq j \leq n_p$). Next, a new unified node N is created with the N_j as children
   and with the appropriate associated conditions. */

conditions := ∅;

```
For each M in Mlist do
    conditions := conditions ∪ CONDITION(M.prod_label)
endFor;
```

N := createNode(p, N_1, ..., N_{n_p}, conditions);

```
return(true)
end;
```

Figure 4-7:   The tree unification algorithm, continued

2. unifyTree(P, R′) returns the value true, and

3. the semantic tree of SEM rooted at R′ is valid and evaluates to s.

Let us examine the evaluation process for the string 'a³b³c³' in the inverted GRIF of figure 4-5. Figure 4-8 gives the parse tree and the unified semantic tree for this string. A more realistic usage of a GRIF is presented in section 4.2.

4.1.4. A proof of correctness

This section will show that the translation specified by an inverted GRIF is actually the inverse of the translation specified by the original GRIF. This will involve several preliminary definitions and propositions.

The reason for introducing the concept of a complete trans set into the definition of GRIFs was given intuitively by proposition 2. That proposition states that every node in a semantic tree of a GRIF *contributes* to the translation. Similarly, the notion of a complete trans set insures that in an inverted GRIF tree, enough information is present to recover the original tree.

Let PT be a parse tree for an inverted GRIF. Let $T = \{XA_1, ..., XA_r\}$ be the labels of a set of nodes of PT. If the nonterminals in T correspond to a complete trans set of the nonterminal X (in the original GRIF), then the set of nodes can be unified into a single node as they capture enough information to recover the original tree. The following definitions and proposition will make this idea more precise.

Let G be a GRIF and $[p_{A_t}: X_0A ::= \beta_0 \ X_{i_{j_1}}Q_{j1} \ \beta_1 \ X_{i_{j_2}}Q_{j2} \ ... \ X_{i_{j_v}}Q_{jv} \ \beta_v]$ be a production of PRODS such that $CANONICAL(p_{A_t}) = [p: X_0 ::= \alpha_0 \ X_1 \ \alpha_1 \ X_2 ... \ X_{n_p} \ \alpha_{n_p}]$. Each one of the right hand side nonterminals in p_{A_t} corresponds to the trans attribute of some right hand side nonterminal in p. Let $RHS\_SYMS(p_{A_t}) = \{X_m \mid \exists \ X_{i_{jk}}Q_{jk}$ on the right hand side of p_{A_t} such that $X_{i_{jk}}Q_{jk}$ is an inverted X_m symbol in p}. $RHS\_SYMS(p_{A_t})$ gives those nonterminals in p which have a trans attribute contributing to the token permuting clause defining X_0.transA. This

The parse tree for 'a³b³c³' :

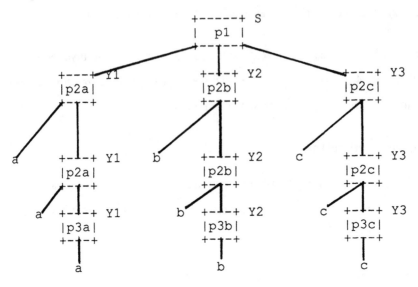

The unified semantic tree:

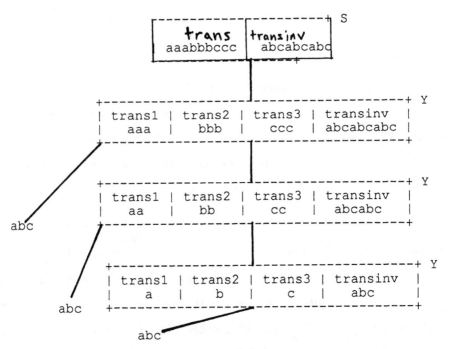

Figure 4-8: A parse tree for a³b³c³ and its unified semantic tree

definition can be expanded to a $\underline{\text{set}}$ of inverted p productions: Let $R = \{p_1, ..., p_z\}$ be a set of productions in PRODS, such that $CANONICAL(p_i) = p$ for all i, $1 \leq i \leq z$. Then $RHS\_SYMS(R) = \cup_{p_i \in R} RHS\_SYMS(p_i)$.

For a production $[p_{A_t}: X_0A ::= \beta_0 \, X_{i_{j1}} Q_{j1} \, \beta_1 \, X_{i_{j2}} Q_{j2} ... X_{i_{jv}} Q_{jv} \, \beta_v]$ in PRODS, let $LHS\_TRANS(p_{A_t}) = X_0.\text{transA}$, where X_0A is the nonterminal in PRODS corresponding to the trans attribute $X_0.\text{transA}$ in G. This definition can likewise be extended to a set of productions: let $R = \{p_1, ..., p_z\}$ be a set of productions in PRODS such that $CANONICAL(p_i) = p$ for all i, $1 \leq i \leq z$. Then $LHS\_TRANS(R) = \cup_{p_i \in R} LHS\_TRANS(p_i)$.

Proposition 3: Let $R = \{p_1, ..., p_z\}$ be a set of productions in PRODS such that $CANONICAL(p_i) = [p: X_0 ::= \alpha_0 X_1 \alpha_1 X_2 ... X_{n_p} \alpha_{n_p}]$ for all i, $1 \leq i \leq z$. If $LHS\_TRANS(R) =$ is a complete trans set for X_0, then $RHS\_SYMS(R) = \{X_1, X_2, ..., X_{n_p}\}$.

In words, if the left hand sides of a group of inverted productions corresponds to a complete trans set, then the right hand side of these productions will include each nonterminal of the right hand side of the original production.

Proof: Let T_k be those trans attributes of X_k that contribute to the token permuting clause defining some trans attribute $X_0.\text{transA}$ in p, such that $X_0.\text{transA}$ is in $LHS\_TRANS(R)$. To prove the proposition, it suffices to show that each T_k ($1 \leq k \leq n_p$) is not empty. This is due to the following fact: if $X_k.\text{transC}$ is in T_k, then $X_k.\text{transC}$ is a string argument to some token permuting clause h_A defining the attribute $X_0.\text{transA}$. But then the inverted X_k symbol X_kC will be on the right hand side of any production p_{A_t} corresponding to some clause of the token permuting clause h_A. Hence X_k will be in $RHS\_SYMS(p_{A_t})$.

To see that each T_k is not empty, recall that, by the definition of GRIFs, $ARGS_p(k)$ is not empty. Say that $X_k.\text{transC} \in ARGS_p(k)$. If $X_k.\text{transC}$ defines some attribute in $LHS\_TRANS(R)$ then the X_k is in T_k. Otherwise $X_k.\text{transC}$ must define an attribute $X_k.\text{transB}$ not in $LHS\_TRANS(R)$. But since $LHS\_TRANS(R)$ is a complete trans set for X_0, by the definition of a complete trans set, there exists some attribute $X_0.transA$ in LHS_TRANS(R) such that $X_0.transA$ COVER $X_0.transB$. By the definition of the COVER relation, there exists an attribute $X_k.transD$ such that $X_k.transD$ is a string attribute to the token permuting clause defining $X_0.transA$ in p. Therefore $X_k.transD$ is in T_k. **End of proof.**

Using this proposition, the following statement establishes an important fact concerning the unification algorithm.

Proposition 4: Let unifyNodes(Mlist, N′) = true, Mlist ≠ ∅, and, for any M ∈ Mlist, CANONICAL(M.prod_label) = [p: $X_0 ::= \alpha_0 X_1 \alpha_1 X_2 ... X_{n_p} \alpha_{n_p}$], $n_p \geq 1$. Then $Mlist_k \neq \emptyset$ ($1 \leq k \leq n_p$). (Where $Mlist_k$ is the set constructed during the function call unifyNodes.)

Proof: Let R = {p_{A_t} | M ∈ Mlist and M.prod_label = p_{A_t}}. The set S constructed in the unification algorithm is the same as the set LHS_TRANS(R). Since the set T is a complete trans set, by proposition 3, RHS_SYMS(R) = {$X_1, ..., X_{n_p}$}. This means that for every X_k ($1 \leq k \leq n_p$), there is some child M′ of a node in Mlist such that M′ is an inverted X_k symbol in p. Hence $Mlist_k$ will not be empty. **End of proof.**

The rest of this section proves that the inversion algorithm is correct: the generated G^{-1} = (PRODS, SEM) will actually be the inverse of the GRIF G. The proof is broken down into three parts. First it is shown that if a parse tree PT in PRODS unifies to a tree ST′, then ST′ is a derivation tree in SEM. In other words, the tree returned from a successful call to unifyTree is really a derivation tree in SEM and that it therefore makes sense to talk of evaluating the tree using the semantics in SEM. Secondly, it will be shown that if there exists a parse tree deriving the string m in PRODS and this parse tree successfully unifies to a tree in SEM which evaluate to s, then there will exist a tree in G translating s to m. Finally it will be shown that if there exists a tree in G translating s to m, then there will exist a parse tree in PRODS deriving m, unifying to a valid tree in SEM which evaluates to s.

Lemma 5: Let P be the root of a derivation tree in PT. If unifyTree(P,R′)=true, then R′ is the root of a derivation tree in SEM.

Proof: For any grammar G, T is said to be a *sub-derivation* tree in G if there exists a derivation tree in G having T as a subtree. (T is like a derivation tree except that the label of its root node is not necessarily the start symbol S). The following proof will show that if the subroutine call unifyNodes(Mlist, N') = true and Mlist $\neq \varnothing$, then N' is the root of a sub-derivation tree in SEM. This will imply that if unifyTree(P, R') = true, R' is a derivation tree in SEM, since R' will be labeled by the start symbol in SEM. The proof of this claim will use induction on the height of the tallest node in Mlist. For the basis step, let the tallest node in Mlist be of height 1. For any node M $\in$ Mlist, M will be labeled by some production $[p_{A_t}: X ::= \beta]$, $\beta \in \Delta^*$. This means that CANONICAL(p_{A_t}) must be of the form [p: X ::= α] and therefore the node N' returned by the function will be a node deriving the string α, with N'.sym_label = X and N'.prod_label = p. Hence N' will be a sub-derivation tree in SEM. For the inductive step, let M, the tallest node in Mlist, be of height h + 1 and let CANONICAL(M.prod_label) = [p: $X_0 ::= \alpha_0 X_1 \alpha_1 X_2 ... X_{n_p} \alpha_{n_p}$]. All the children of the nodes in Mlist will be of at most height h. By proposition 4, each Mlist$_j \neq \varnothing$ ($1 \leq j \leq n_p$) and by induction, each call to unifyNode(Mlist$_j$, N$_j$) will return a sub-derivation tree in SEM rooted at the node N$_j$, where N$_j$.sym_label = X$_j$. Hence the node N' returned by the function will be a node having children α_0, N$_1$, α_1, ..., N$_{n_p}$, α_{n_p}, with N.sym_label = X_0 and N.prod_label = p. Therefore N' will be a sub-derivation tree in SEM. **End of proof.**

Lemma 6: Let PT be a parse tree in PRODS deriving m unifying to the valid semantic tree ST' in SEM evaluating to s. Then there exists a valid semantic tree ST in G computing the translation (s, m).

Proof: For any valid tree ST' in SEM there exists an valid isomorphic semantic tree ST in G. ST' and ST differ only in that every node N' in ST' has an additional attribute field N'.transinv not found at the corresponding node N in ST. Since each node N in ST will have the same semantics as associated with its corresponding node N' in ST' (except for the semantics associated with the transinv attribute), all the corresponding attribute values in these trees will be equal. Furthermore, a simple inductive argument will show that for any nonterminal node N' in ST', N' derives the string q iff N'.transinv $= q$.

Let R' be the root of ST' and R be the root of its corresponding isomorphic semantic tree ST in G. Since, by assumption, R'.transinv $= s$, R' must derive s. Since the trees ST and ST' are isomorphic, R must also derive s. Hence, to complete the proof of the lemma, it only needs to be shown that R.trans $=m$. Since ST and ST' are isomorphic, it suffices to show that R'.trans $=m$.

A node M in PT is said to *unify* to a node N' in ST' if, during some call to unifyNodes(Mlist, N) (during tree unification of PT to ST'), $M \in$ Mlist and $N' = N$.

Assume that during a call to unifyNodes, the function equalTrees(Z1, Z2) is called. If this function returns true, then Z1 and Z2 are identical subtrees, and there exists a one-to-one correspondence between nodes in Z1's subtree and nodes in Z2's subtree. Let M1 be a node in Z1's subtree and M2 be the corresponding node in Z2's subtree. We then say that M1 *subsumes* M2. During tree unification of PT to ST', every node M in PT is either unified to some node N' in ST' or is subsumed by some other node in PT. Furthermore, any node in PT is unified to at most one node in ST'.

Define the mapping μ from nodes of PT to trans attributes in ST' as follows:

$$\mu(M) = \begin{cases} N'.\text{transA, if M unifies to } N', N'.\text{sym\_label} = X, \text{ and M.sym\_label} = XA. \\ \mu(M1), \text{ if M is subsumed by M1.} \end{cases}$$

Given a trans attribute N.transA of a semantic tree, let value(N.transA) denote the value assigned to N.transA in the computation of the semantic tree. It will now be shown that for any node M of PT, if M derives q then value($\mu(M)$) $= q$. If M is subsumed by M1, both M and M1 derive the same string and it therefore suffices to show that the above statement holds for unsubsumed nodes of PT. The proof is by induction on the height of the unsubsumed node M in PT. Let M be of height 1 and let $\mu(M) = N'.\text{transA}$. Then M.prod_label $= [p_{A_i}: X_0A ::= \beta]$, where $\beta \in \Delta^*$. The token permuting function defining N'.transA is of the form: $<X_0$.transA $=$ if $g_1(...)$ then ... elsif $g_t(...)$ then β else ...$>$. Since CONDITION$(p_{A_t}) = <$NOT$(g_1(...))$ AND ... AND $g_t(...)>$ is attached to N' and evaluates to true, N'.transA will equal β. Hence M derives β and value$(\mu(M)) = \beta$.

For the inductive step, let M be of height $h + 1$, $\mu(M) = N'$.transA, CANONICAL(M.prod_label) $= [p: X_0 ::= \alpha_0 X_1 \alpha_1 X_2 ... X_{n_p} \alpha_{n_p}]$ and M.prod_label $= [p_{A_t}: X_0 A ::= \beta_0 X_{i_{j1}} Q_{j1} \beta_1 ... X_{i_{jv}} Q_{jv} \beta_v]$. Let $M_{i_{jr}} Q_{jr}$ be the son of M corresponding to $X_{i_{jr}} Q_{jr}$ $(1 \leq r \leq v)$ and let t_r be the string that $M_{i_{jr}} Q_{jr}$ derives. Then M derives the string "$\beta_0 t_1 \beta_1 ... t_v \beta_v$". The token permuting function computing N'.transA is of the form: $<X_0$.transA $=$ if $g_1(...)$ then ... elsif $g_t(...)$ then Concatenate$(\beta_0, X_{i_{j1}}$.transQ$_{j1}, \beta_1, ..., X_{i_{jv}}$.transQ$_{jv}, \beta_v)$ else ...$>$. Let $N_1, ..., N_{n_p}$ be the children of N' corresponding to $X_1, ..., X_{n_p}$. Since CONDITION$(p_{A_t}) = <$NOT$(g_1(...))$ AND ... AND $g_t(...)>$ is attached to N' and evaluates to true, N'.transA $=$ Concatenate$(\beta_0, N_{i_{j1}}$.transQ$_{j1}, \beta_1, ..., N_{i_{jv}}$.transQ$_{jv}, \beta_v)$. Since $\mu(M_{i_{jr}} Q_{jr}) = N_{i_{jr}}$.transQ$_{jr}$ $(1 \leq r \leq v)$, N'.transA $=$ Concatenate$(\beta_0,$ value$(\mu(M_{i_{j1}} Q_{j1})), \beta_1, ...,$ value$(\mu(M_{i_{jv}} Q_{jv})), \beta_v)$. However, since each node $M_{i_{jr}} Q_{jr}$ $(1 \leq r \leq v)$ is of height $\leq h$, by induction, value$(\mu(M_{i_{jr}} Q_{jr})) = t_r$. Hence N'.transA $=$ "$\beta_0 t_1 \beta_1 ... t_v \beta_v$". This completes the proof that if M derives q, value$(\mu(M)) = q$. Let P be the root of root of PT and R' the root of ST$'$. P derives m implies that value$(\mu(P)) =$ value$(R'$.trans$) = m$. This proves the lemma. **End of proof.**

Lemma 7: Let ST be a valid semantic tree in G computing the translation (s, m). Then there exists a parse tree PT in PRODS deriving m unifying to the valid semantic tree ST$'$ in SEM such that ST$'$ evaluates to s.

Proof: Given the semantic tree ST in G, create a parse tree PT in PRODS as follows:

1. For each node N in ST, mark those trans attributes of N which contribute to the translation R.trans (where R is the root node of ST).

2. Starting at the leaf nodes of ST and working one's way up the tree, for each marked attribute transA of a node N, where N.sym_label $= X$ and N.prod_label $= p$, create a node M in PT with M.sym_label $= XA$.

3. If N.transA is computed by the token permuting function f_t (the tth clause of the token permuting clause computing X.transA in p), then let M.prod_label $= p_{A_t}$.

4. Make the children of M be those nodes already created in PT (recall that if N is the parent of N′, M and M′ are nodes in PT corresponding to attributes of N and N′ respectively, then M′ is created before M) which correspond to the trans attributes used in the token permuting function f_t.

5. Permute the order of these children and add terminal nodes as required to make M the root of an instance of the production p_{A_t}.

6. If several marked trans attributes of N, $N.transA_1$, ...,$N.transA_k$ are computed by token permuting functions which take the same argument N′.transB, then the nodes M_1, ..., M_k of PT corresponding to $N.transA_1$, ..., $N.transA_k$ all require the same child M′, the node of PT corresponding to N′.transB. In such a case duplicate the subtree rooted at M′ k times and make each M_r $(1 \leq r \leq k)$ a parent of one such subtree. Similarly, if N′.transB appears as an argument k times to the token permuting function computing some marked attribute N.transA, then duplicate the subtree rooted at M′ in PT k times and make each copy a child of M, where M′ and M are the nodes in PT corresponding to N′.transB and N.transA respectively.

The tree PT created as above (i) is a parse tree in PRODS deriving m and (ii) unifies to a valid semantic tree ST′ in SEM, computing the translation s. It is easy to see that PT is a valid parse tree in PRODS. To see that it derives m, it suffices to show that for any marked attribute N.transA in ST such that N.transA = q, the corresponding node M in PT derives q. If this is the case, then since R.trans = m, where R is the root node of ST, P derives m, where P the root node of PT.

This claim will be proved using induction on height of the node N in ST. If N is of height 1, then N.sym_label = [p: X ::= α], $\alpha \in \Sigma^*$ and N.transA is defined by some token permuting function f_t of the form $f_t() = \beta$, $\beta \in \Delta^*$. Then M.prod_label = [p_{A_t}: X ::= β]. This proves the basis step. For the inductive step, let N be a node in ST of height h + 1. Let N.prod_label = [p: X_0 ::= $\alpha_0 X_1 \alpha_1 X_2 ... X_{n_p} \alpha_{n_p}$] and the marked attribute N.transA be defined by some token permuting function $f_t(X_{i1}.transQ_1,...,X_{iv}.transQ_v) =$ Concatenate(β_0, $X_{i_{j1}}.transQ_{j1}$, $\beta_1 X_{i_{j2}}.transQ_{j2}$, ..., $X_{i_{jv}}.transQ_{jv}$, β_v). Let $N_{i_{jr}}.transQ_{jr}$ $(1 \leq r \leq v)$ be the attribute in ST corresponding to $X_{i_{jr}}.transQ_{jr}$, $M_{i_{jr}}Q_{jr}$ be the node in PT corresponding to $N_{i_{jr}}.transQ_{jr}$, and t_r be the string derived by $M_{i_{jr}}Q_{jr}$. Then M.prod_label = p_{A_t} and M derives the string "$\beta_0 t_1 \beta_1 t_2...t_v \beta_v$". N.transA = Concatenate(β_0, $N_{i_{j1}}.transQ_{j1}$, β_1, $N_{i_{j2}}.transQ_{j2}$, ..., $N_{i_{jv}}.transQ_{jv}$, β_v). But by induction,

$N_{i_{jr}}.transQ_{jr} = t_r$ ($1 \leq r \leq v$), since each node N_{jr} is of height at most h. Hence M derives the string given in N.transA.

To see that PT unifies to a valid semantic tree ST′ evaluating to s, the result of running the algorithm unifyTree on PT must be analyzed. A complete analysis is left to the reader. The following is a brief sketch of the proof that ST′ is valid and evaluates to s:

First of all, note that the algorithm to unify trees essentially undoes the actions used to create the tree PT. Formally, if Mlist is a set of nodes in PT corresponding <u>exactly</u> to the marked trans attributes of some node N in ST, then (i) unifyNodes(Mlist, N′) = true and (ii) the subtree (in ST′) rooted at N′ will be isomorphic with the subtree (in ST) rooted at N. Furthermore, (iii) the conditions attached to N′ will be conditions that are related to the token permuting clauses computing the marked trans attributes of N and evaluate to true. The proof of this claim can make use of induction of the height of the node N in ST. The following fact is useful in the proof: If M_1, ..., M_z are the nodes in PT corresponding to the marked trans attributes $N.transA_1$, ..., $N.transA_z$ of a node N in ST and N.sym_label = X, then $\{X.transA_1, ..., X.transA_z\}$ is a complete trans set for X. This is true since ST is a semantic tree in G and G is GRIF grammar. Since the created tree ST′ is isomorphic to ST, for any node N′ in ST′, N′.transinv = q iff N, its corresponding node in ST, derives q. (This can easily be shown to be true by induction). Hence R′.transinv (where R′ is the root of ST′) will equal s. **End of proof.**

Theorem 8: Let G be a GRIF describing the translation T and G^{-1} = (PRODS,SEM) be its inverse (obtained by running the GRIF inversion algorithm on G) describing the translation T^{-1}. Then (s, m) is in T iff (m, s) is in T^{-1}.

Proof: The proof follows directly from lemmas 6 and 7. **End of proof.**

4.2. Summary and additional remarks

The GRIF grammars introduced in this chapter are a generalized version of RIFs. They were introduced in order to make it easier to write efficient invertible specifications. To this end, they allow the use of multiple trans attributes and relax the restrictions on token permuting clauses. This generalization, however, requires a more sophisticated process for evaluating strings in the inverse grammar. In between parsing and semantic tree evaluation a new process, called tree unification, has to be performed. This process takes the parse tree and unifies many nodes into a single one, thereby creating a semantic tree isomorphic to the "original" semantic tree (the one that would have produced the parse string as output).

To illustrate the usefulness of GRIFs in a practical setting, consider the problem of translating a Pascal write statement to a C printf statement. Such a translation would, for instance, translate the Pascal string "write('enter number', Y)" to the C equivalent "printf("%s%d", "enter number", Y)". The reason why this is difficult to express as a RIF is because, for each argument to the write statement, two translations must be captured. The first gives the control argument, the second gives the actual translation. However this can be expressed quite simply as a GRIF, as illustrated by figure 4-9.

The inversion of this GRIF would result in the parsing productions PRODS and canonical productions SEM of figure 4-10. The reader is invited to draw the parse tree for the C string "printf("%s%d", "enter number", Y)" and to find the semantic tree the unification algorithm would produce for this parse tree.

The following few paragraphs compare GRIFs to other known grammar based translation methodologies and provide some additional comments concerning the evaluation of inverted GRIFs.

1. It is interesting to note the relationship between GRIFs and the attribute coupled grammars (ACGs) [23, 25], especially when restricting ACGs to allow only synthesized syntactic attributes. On one hand, ACGs are more general than GRIFs in that they do

p_1: writeStmt ::= write (args).
  writeStmt.trans = concat['printf ("', args.transA, '",',
                    args.transB, ')'];
  args.env = writeStmt.env;

p_2: $args_0$ ::= $args_1$, arg.
  $args_0$.transA = concat($args_1$.transA, arg.transA);
  $args_0$.transB = concat($args_1$.transB, ',', arg.transB);
  $args_1$.env = $args_0$.env;
  arg.env = $args_0$.env;

p_3: args ::= arg.
  args.transA = arg.transA;
  args.transB = arg.transB;
  arg.env = args.env;

p_4: arg ::= expression.
  arg.transA = if expression.type = intType then '%d'
    elsif expression.type = charType then '%c'
    elsif expression.type = stringType then '%s'
    ... ;
  arg.transB = expression.trans;
  expression.env = arg.env;

Figure 4-9: A GRIF

not require every symbol to have a syntactic attribute, whereas in GRIFs every nonterminal must have least one trans attribute. On the other hand, a trans attribute in a GRIF may contribute to several token permuting clauses, whereas a syntactic attribute in an ACG may only contribute to one syntactic function. It would be very interesting to see whether GRIFs can be generalized even further to allow inherited trans attributes, just as ACGs allow inherited syntactic attributes.

2. It is also interesting to note the relationship between the inversion of GRIFs and the inversion of *General Syntax-Directed Translation Schema* (GSDTS) in [52]. If one strips multiple trans AGs of all attributes other than the trans attributes, and requires that each trans attribute be defined by a token permuting function instead of a token permuting clause, the result is a GSDTS. Hence GSDTS are much more restricted than GRIFs. For this reason a very efficient algorithm for finding valid parses in the "inverse GSDTS" is possible. Essentially this algorithm builds a unified parse tree during parsing. If it succeeds, then it can easily recover the original tree, as there are no

The parsing productions PRODS:

p_1: writeStmt ::= printf (" argsA " , argsB).

p_{2_A}: $argsA_0$ ::= $argsA_1$ argA.

p_{2_B}: $argsB_0$ ::= $argsB_1$, argB.

p_{3_A}: argsA ::= argA.

p_{3_B}: argsB ::= argB.

$p_{4_{A1}}$: argA ::= %d.

$p_{4_{A2}}$: argA ::= %c.

$p_{4_{A3}}$: argA ::= %s.

p_{4_B}: argB ::= expression.

The canonical productions SEM:

p_1: writeStmt ::= write (args).
   writeStmt.trans = concat['printf ("', args.transA, '",',
                  args.transB, ')'];
   args.env = writeStmt.env;
   writeStmt.transinv = concat['write', '(', args.transinv, ')'];

p_2: $args_0$ ::= $args_1$, arg.
   $args_0$.transA = concat($args_1$.transA, arg.transA);
   $args_0$.transB = concat($args_1$.transB, arg.transB);
   $args_1$.env = $args_0$.env;
   arg.env = $args_0$.env;
   $args_0$.transinv = concat[$args_1$, ',', arg];

p_3: args ::= arg.
   args.transA = arg.transA;
   args.transB = arg.transB;
   arg.env = args.env;
   args.transinv = arg.transinv;

p_4: arg ::= expression.
   arg.transA = if expression.type = intType then '%d'
      elsif expression.type = charType then '%c'
      elsif expression.type = stringType then '%s'
      ... ;
   arg.transB = expression.trans;
   expression.env = arg.env;
   arg.transinv = expression.transinv;

Figure 4-10: The inverted GRIF

other semantics associated with GSDTS. What this chapter calls tree unification is very similar to what Reiss calls finding a common parse.

3. GRIFs require a two stage process to build the semantic tree: first to build the parse tree in PRODS and then to unify it to a tree in SEM. As done for inverse GSDTS in [52], it is possible to combine the parsing stage with the tree unification stage. This would allow one to more rapidly rule out non-valid parses that fail tree unification.

4. RIFs could have been originally formulated as a pair (PRODS, SEM) just as GRIFs were formulated. This would have made the generalization from RIFs to GRIFs more natural. However, for RIFs it is unnecessary to introduce all the extra machinery of tree unification as required for GRIFs. This is because in RIFs, if $CANONICAL(p_{A_t}) = p$, then p_{A_t} and p are isomorphic in structure. This implies that the inverse parse tree will be isomorphic to the original, making tree unification unnecessary; i.e., all the semantics of p can be applied to p_{A_t} without unification, something which is not true for GRIFs.

5. To make the implementation of GRIFs more efficient, one can combine the attribute evaluation stage with the evaluation of semantic conditions. This can be done as follows: instead of associating a single production p in SEM with every production p in the original GRIF G, one can associate many productions in SEM with each production p in G. Each one of these productions will be identical except for the fact that they will encode different semantic conditions into their semantic equations. During the tree unification algorithm, instead of attaching the semantic conditions to the unified node, the algorithm will label the node by the production which encodes these conditions in its semantic equations. In particular, let X_0, the left-part symbol in p, have k trans attributes. Let the token permuting clause associated with $X_0.transA$ ($1 \leq i \leq k$) in p have C_A "clauses"; i.e., it is of the form: $<X_0.transA = $ if $ERROR(...)$ or $g_1(...)$ then ERROR elsif $g_2(...)$ then $f_2(...)$ ... else $f_{C_A}(...)>$. Let $CLAUSE(C^A_t)$ ($1 \leq t \leq C_A$) equal $<not(g_1(...))$ and ... and $not(g_{t-1}(...))$ and $g_t(...)>$ if $t \geq 1$ and let it equal the constant boolean value "true" otherwise. Then create $C_1 \times C_2 \times ... \times C_k$ productions $\{p_{j_1, j_2, ..., j_k}$ | for $1 \leq A \leq k$, $1 \leq j_A \leq C_A\}$ in SEM for each production p in G. If p is of the form

[p: $X_0 ::= \alpha_0 X_1 \alpha_1 X_2 \ldots X_{n_p} \alpha_{n_p}$], then $p_{j_1, j_2, \ldots, j_k}$ will be of the form [p: $X_0 ::= \alpha_0 X_1 \alpha_1 X_2 \ldots X_{n_p} \alpha_{n_p}$] and will have all the semantics that are associated with p. In addition it will have one additional semantic function of the form: $<X_0.\text{transinv} = \text{if not}(\text{CLAUSE}(C^1_{j_1})$ and $\ldots$ and $\text{CLAUSE}(C^k_{j_k}))$ then ERROR else Concatenate$(\alpha_0, X_1.\text{transinv}, \ldots, X_{n_p}.\text{transinv}, \alpha_{n_p})>$. During unification of the parse tree, instead of attaching conditions to a node N, one must choose the appropriate production $p_{j_1 j_2, \ldots j_k}$ which incorporates the conditions into the semantic function computing $X_0.\text{transinv}$.

6. Sometimes in an inverted GRIF there will be an ambiguous parse which can be resolved by tree unification. That is, there may be two or more parses of a subtree, only one which can be unified into a valid tree. This disambiguation can be efficiently incorporated into the tree unification algorithm itself, by allowing the unambiguous parse of one subtree to aid in choosing the the correct parse of a subtree with which it is being unified.

This chapter has explored an important generalization to RIFs: the usage of multiple trans attributes. We have shown how to invert these generalized RIFs and how to build an attribute evaluation system for them, employing a tree unifier. This concludes the first part of the thesis, detailing the theory of AG inversion. The rest of this thesis will focus on how to apply the inversion technique to build source-to-source translators and how to actually implement the inversion algorithm. The next chapter begins this discussion by providing an overview to INVERT. The INVERT system implements the inversion algorithm of chapter 3, but also contains many extensions aimed at making it easier to write bi-directional translators. Some of these extensions provide RIFs with capabilities similar to GRIFs, while avoiding the overhead of tree unification. In this way the original and inverted AGs can be run in a traditional AG-based evaluation environment.

Chapter 5

The INVERT system

Based on the ideas of AG inversion, I have created the INVERT system [65]. It accepts a restricted AG as input and delivers the inverted AG as output, as indicated in figure 5-1.

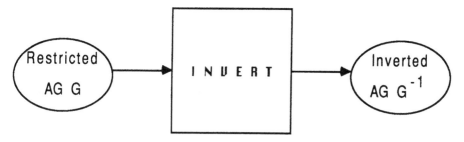

Figure 5-1: The INVERT system

The INVERT system itself is written as an attribute grammar, specifying the translation from restricted AGs to inverse AGs. The INVERT translator was then obtained by running the AG through the Linguist [19] AG-based translator-writing-system. The INVERT AG is 1537 lines long, has 54 nonterminal symbols, 150 attributes, 115 productions, and 327 semantic rules. It is evaluable in 3 alternating passes.

The restrictions placed on the input AG are basically those of RIFs, as described in chapter 2. The inversion algorithm embodied in INVERT is basically the inversion algorithm for RIFs, given in chapter 3. However, as pointed out in the last chapter, the restrictions required by RIFs are often too severe in practice if one desires to write useful and complex translators. For this reason, INVERT will accept a generalized version of RIFs, and the inversion algorithm embodied in INVERT subsumes the algorithm of chapter 3. In addition, the INVERT system contains a postprocessor which helps to eliminate syntactic ambiguity from the inverted AG.

The rest of this chapter elaborates on the INVERT system. The first part of this chapter will outline the extensions to RIFs permitted by INVERT and explains adaptions to the inversion algorithm to deal with these generalizations. It also provides many "real-life" examples, drawn from my Pascal-to-C and C-to-Pascal translators, demonstrating these techniques. The chief way in which INVERT differs from the pure RIF paradigm of chapter 2 is that INVERT will accept RIFs employing a generalized form of token permuting function. One generalization, described in the following section, is intended to give RIFs some of the expressive power found in GRIFs of the last chapter. Another extension to token permuting functions allows the AG writer to use out-of-line semantic functions when defining the trans attribute. It is presented in section 5.2. The second part of this chapter discusses two mechanisms used by INVERT to rid ambiguity from the generated inverse grammar. One mechanism is a postprocessor which automatically removes ambiguity that can be detected statically. The second mechanism allows the user to specify that certain syntax and semantics should not be generated in the inverse AG. These features are discussed in the last section of the chapter.

5.1. Additive and deletive token permuting functions

At first the INVERT system required that the input grammar correspond to pure RIFs. However, as I began to use the system to write real and nontrivial translations, it soon became apparent that this form was too restricted. A common problem that arose was the difficulty in couching translations in terms of token permuting functions. Although a way to do so could always eventually be found, it often required the introduction of awkward and unnatural constructs. Besides making the RIFs unpleasant to use, these constructs also introduced unnecessary ambiguity into the original and inverted RIFs.

This section presents two complementary extensions to RIFs, *additive token permuting functions* and *deletive token permuting functions.* The former will extend token permuting functions so that more than just the trans attributes of the right-part symbols can be arguments to the function. The latter will extend token permuting functions so that not every right-part trans attribute <u>must</u> be an argument to the function. These extensions will allow the AG writer to specify translations that are similar to GRIFs. As in GRIFs, the original and inverse semantic trees specified by these extended RIFs will no longer be isomorphic to one another. This similarity between additive and deletive token permuting functions and GRIFs is not coincidental: after experimenting with additive and deletive token permuting functions in the INVERT system, I attempted to devise a general and cohesive formalism for expressing the types of translations performed by these extensions. The result of this investigation was the GRIF formalism of the last chapter. For this reason the reader will notice that many of the examples of this section employing additive and deletive token permuting functions could be expressed in a more natural fashion using GRIFs. Nonetheless, there are some important distinctions between additive and deletive token permuting functions on the one hand and GRIFs on the other hand. First of all, additive and deletive token permuting functions require more user input than GRIFs. Secondly, additive and deletive token permuting functions do not require the extra stage of tree unification required by GRIFs, and can therefore be run in a traditional AG environment. Finally, the two formalisms are not entirely equivalent; as we shall see, there are some translations that can be performed by additive and deletive token permuting functions that cannot be performed very easily using GRIFs.

5.1.1. Additive token permuting functions

Figure 5-2 gives an example AG, expressing the translation from a Pascal-like language, requiring procedure headings of the form: "procedure-name (parameters-name-and-type)" to a C-like language requiring headings of the form: "procedure-name (parameter-names) parameter-names-and-types". For example, it would translate the string "f(a, b: integer; c: real)" to the string "f(a, b, c) int a, b; real c;".

p_1: procDec ::= Id (parameters).
   procDec.trans = Concatenate(Id.trans, '(', genParams(parameters.list), ')',
    parameters.trans);

p_2: parameters0 ::= parameters1 ; parameter.
   parameters0.trans = Concatenate(parameters1.trans, ';', parameter.trans);
   parameters0.list = Union(parameters1.list, parameter.list);

p_3: parameter ::= identifiers : type.
   parameter.trans = Concatenate(type.trans, identifiers.trans);
   parameter.list = identifiers.list;

p_4: identifiers0 ::= identifiers1 , Id.
   identifiers0.trans = Concatenate(identifiers1.trans, ',', Id.trans);
   identifiers0.list = Union(identifiers1.list, listOf(Id.trans));

Figure 5-2: An additive token permuting function

In this example, the function genParams takes a set of identifiers {id1, id2, ..., idn} and generates the string "id1, id2, ..., idn". A string of identifiers in this form is called an ID-LIST. Although it is an easy exercise to rewrite this AG fragment as a GRIF- the attribute list would be replaced by a second trans attribute- this grammar fails to be a RIF. This is because the use of the function genParams in production p_1 makes the function defining procDec.trans <u>not</u> a token permuting function. In pure RIFs, the function defining a trans attribute must be a token permuting function in order for the inversion algorithm to know how to invert it. In this case the inversion algorithm cannot get a handle on how to represent the strings genParams produces in the inverted context-free production pI_1; the inverted production must be of the form [pI_1: procDecI ::= IdI (X) parametersI] where X represents strings that genParams could produce. Unfortunately, the inversion algorithm doesn't know what to place in the position occupied by X.

To solve this problem, the inversion algorithm must be provided with
    1. knowledge about the primitive types (domains) employed by the semantic
       functions of the RIF grammar and

    2. knowledge on how to derive strings over this domain using context-free
       productions.

In particular, for the example given above, the inversion algorithm would need to know
    1. that genParams is a function whose range is ID-LIST and

2. the syntax of an ID-LIST.

Using this information, it could invert the productions of figure 5-2, producing the inverse productions of figure 5-3. Note that pI_1 introduces a new nonterminal, IdList, and that productions pI_5 - pI_6 are needed to produce strings that IdList can derive. This new nonterminal has a distinguished attribute IdList.value, which takes on the value of the string derived by this nonterminal (e.g., if IdList derives 'a, b', then IdList.value = 'a, b'). The semantics of the inverse production pI_1 enforces the relationship that the string derived from the nonterminal IdList (given in IdList.value) must equal genParams(parameters.list), as required by the original production p_1.

pI_1: procDecI ::= IdI (IdList) parametersI.
    procDec.transinv = if IdList.value ≠ genParams(parametersI.list)
        then ERROR
        else Concatenate(IdI.transinv, '(', parametersI.transinv, ')');

pI_2: parametersI0 ::= parametersI1 ; parameterI.
    parametersI0.transinv = Concatenate(parametersI1.transinv, ';',
                    parameter.trans);
    parametersI0.list = Union(parametersI1.list, parameterI.list);

pI_3: parameterI ::= typeI identifiersI.
    parameterI.transinv = Concatenate(identifiersI.transinv,':',typeI.transinv);
    parameterI.list = identifiersI.list;

pI_4: identifiersI0 ::= identifiersI1 , IdI.
    identifiersI0.transinv = Concatenate(identifiersI1.transinv,',', IdI.transinv);
    identifiersI0.list = Union(identifiersI1.list, listOf(IdI.trans));

pI_5: IdList0 ::= IdList1 , IdI.
    IdList0.value = Concatenate(IdList1.value, ',', IdI.value);

pI_6: IdList ::= IdI.
    IdList.value = IdI.value;

Figure 5-3: Its inverse

The technique illustrated by this example can be generalized. A function $f(\delta_1, ..., \delta_n; \gamma)$ is an *additive token permuting function* over an alphabet Δ if and only if it is of the following form: $f(\delta_1, ..., \delta_n; \gamma) = \text{Concatenate}(\beta_0, \delta_{i_1}, \beta_1, \delta_{i_2}, ..., \delta_{i_j}, \beta_j, foo(\gamma),$ $\beta_{j+1}, \delta_{i_{j+1}}, \beta_{j+2}, ..., \delta_{i_n}, \beta_{n+1})$ where each δ_k ($1 \leq k \leq n$) is in Δ^*, $[i_1..i_n]$ is a permutation of $[1..n]$, each β_k ($1 \leq k \leq n$) is a constant in Δ^*, γ is a variable taking on values over some domain D, and foo is a function from the domain D to the range $R \subseteq \Delta^*$. This sort of function is similar to a token permuting function, only it allows the addition of the function foo and the variable γ to play a role in the translation.

To extend RIF grammars, each primitive clause of a token permuting clause is allowed to be an additive token permuting function instead of simply a token permuting function. For simplicity, the following discussion examines the case where the token permuting clause contains a single token permuting function; the ideas stated here can be easily generalized by the reader[17]. Let G be a RIF grammar specifying a translation over $\Sigma \times \Delta$ and let $[p: X_0 ::= \alpha_0 X_1 \alpha_1 X_2 \ldots X_{n_p} \alpha_{n_p}]$ be a production in G with the distinguished semantic function

X_0.trans = if ERROR(X_1.trans, ..., X_{n_p}.trans) then ERROR
    else f(X_1.trans, ..., X_{n_p}.trans; X_u.att)

where f is an additive token permuting function of the form Concatenate(β_0, X_{i_1}.trans, β_1, ..., β_{j-1}, X_{i_j}.trans, β_j, foo(X_u.att), β_{j+1}, $X_{i_{j+1}}$.trans, β_{j+2}, ..., $X_{i_{np}}$.trans, β_{n_p+1}), and foo is a function from domain D to range R. Then p inverts to $[pI: XI_0 ::= \beta_0 XI_{i_1} \beta_1 \cdots \beta_{j-1} \ XI_{i_j} \beta_j \ R \ \beta_{j+1} XI_{i_{j+1}} \ \beta_{j+2} \ldots XI_{i_{np}} \beta_{n_p+1}]$ with the distinguished semantic function

XI_0.trans = if ERROR(XI_{i_1}.transinv,...,$XI_{i_{np}}$.transinv)
        or R.value $\neq$ foo(X_u.att)
    then ERROR
    else Concatenate(α_0, XI_1.transinv, ..., XI_{n_p}.transinv, α_{n_p});

Here R is a new context-free symbol introduced into the inverse grammar deriving strings over the domain R. It has a single attribute, R.value, which gives the value of the string it derives (if R derives the string r, R.value = 'r'). The productions used to derive strings over R can be either supplied by the writer of the RIF grammar, or can be automatically selected from a database by the inversion algorithm. This database would be originally compiled by those implementing the inversion algorithm and would

---

[17]Similarly, the remarks of this section can be generalized to a case where the extended token permuting function contains not only one instance of a function foo, but instances of several functions foo1, foo2, ..., fook. Also, each function foo can take several attributes as arguments, instead of a single argument.

contain knowledge of the syntax of many common domains. The inversion algorithm, however, must be explicitly told that the range of the semantic function foo is R; this information must be included in the specification of the RIF. Ideally, the domain R specified should be as precise as possible. For example, in production p_1 of figure 5-2, the function genParams could be declared to be a function whose range is alpha-numeric strings, instead of a function whose range is ID-LIST (the domain of ID-LIST is strictly contained in the domain of alpha-numeric strings). The former declaration would cause the inverse production to admit as a legal parse any alpha-numeric character string for parameters, even if it is not a valid list of identifiers. Even though such ill-formed parameters would eventually be rejected during semantic analysis, it is more efficient to initially restrict the domain of acceptable parses to those strings with the correct ID-LIST syntax. In general, by declaring the range of the semantic functions as precisely as possible, the generated inverse specifications become more efficient.

By now the reason for the name "additive" token permuting function should be clear: these functions can add new nonterminals to the inverted production. It is left to the reader to show that by allowing additive token permuting functions and using the technique described here to invert such constructs, the generated inverse specification is actual inverse of the original specification; i.e., (x, w) is in T if and only if (w, x) is in T^{-1}.

It is interesting to examine the special case of additive token permuting functions which merely duplicates a trans attribute. An example of this behavior is given in figure 5-4. These productions model a translation from a C-like syntax for assignment statements to a Pascal-like syntax. Assignment statements of the form "Id = expression" get translated to "Id := expression" and assignment statements of the form "Id += expression" get translated to "Id := Id + expression".

The distinguished semantic function of production r1 is not a token permuting function; the first clause duplicates the attribute Id.trans in the output. However it is an additive token permuting function. In this case the "foo" function is merely the identity

r1: assnStmt ::= Id assnOp expression.
    assnStmt.trans = if assnOp.duplicating
        then Concatenate(Id.trans, ':=', Id.trans, assnOp.trans, expression.trans)
        else Concatenate(Id.trans, assnOp.trans, expression.trans);

r2: assnOp ::= =.
    assnOp.trans = ':=';
    assnOp.duplicating = false;

r3: assnOp ::= += | -= | *= | ...
    assnOp.trans = ' + ' | ' - ' | ' * ' | ... ;
    assnOp.duplicating = true;

Figure 5-4: A duplicating token permuting function

function on a single attribute: foo(Id.trans) = identity(Id.trans) = Id.trans. In general, the semantic function Concatenate(..., Xj.trans, ...,Xj.trans, ...) can always be viewed as the additive token permuting function Concatenate(..., Xj.trans, ..., identity(Xj.trans), ...). Furthermore, it is not necessary in this case to specify the range of foo. Since it is the identity function, it will take on values over the domain of X.trans and the nonterminal XI derives strings precisely over that domain. Viewed in this light, it is possible to invert the extended RIF of figure 5-4 to produce the inverted RIF of figure 5-5. The condition of production $rI1_a$ can be expressed as "IdI1.trans ≠ IdI2.trans" instead of "IdI1.trans ≠ IdI2.value" since, for any nonterminal XI in an inverted RIF, XI.trans equals XI.value (i.e., in an inverted RIF, XI.trans gives the string that XI derives and XI.transinv gives its translation).

Additive token permuting functions are implemented in the INVERT system as follows: If an additive token permuting function of the input RIF makes use of a function foo, then a declaration of the range of foo is required. This declaration, provided at the end of the RIF specification, must be of the form: range(foo) = X, where X is a nonterminal symbol deriving strings over the range of foo. If X is a nonterminal of the original RIF this information suffices; otherwise productions deriving strings from X must also be provided.

Although additive token permuting functions were introduced in order to mimic the power of GRIFs, the two are not really comparable. Many translations which can be

$rI1_a$: assnStmtI ::= IdI_1 := IdI_2 assnOpI expressionI.
   assnStmtI.transinv = if IdI_1.trans ≠ IdI_2.trans or
                NOT(assnOpI.duplicating) then ERROR
     else Concatenate(IdI_1.transinv, assnOpI.transinv, expressionI.transinv);

$rI1_b$: assnStmtI ::= IdI assnOpI expressionI.
  assnStmtI.transinv = if assnOpI.duplicating then ERROR
    else Concatenate(IdI.transinv, assnOpI.transinv expressionI.transinv);

rI2: assnOpI ::= :=.
  assnOpI.transinv = '=';
  assnOpI.trans = ':=';
  assnOpI.duplicating = false;

rI3: assnOpI ::= + | - | * | ...
  assnOpI.transinv = '+=' | '-=' | '*=' | ... ;
  assnOpI.trans = ' + ' | ' - ' | ' * ' | ... ;
  assnOpI.duplicating = true;

Figure 5-5: Its inverse

performed effortlessly by GRIFs become much more complicated using additive token permuting functions. Furthermore, the latter introduces extra nontermininals and semantics into the inverse specification. On the other hand, additive token permuting functions can also express translations that are not expressible by GRIFs. This is because, in addition to being able to mimic multiple trans attributes, additive token permuting functions can also be used to write translations that are not "token permuting" in nature. Figure 5-6 gives an example of an additive token permuting function used to express the translation from strings of the form "IF expression THEN statement" to strings of the form "expression FJP LLAB statement LAB LLAB", where FJP is a conditional jump statement, LAB precedes a labeled statement, and LLAB is a label. genLab is function from the domain of integers to the range of labels. As each label following a LAB must be unique, the attribute if_stmt.labnum records the number of labels generated so far and genLab generates a unique label based upon this attribute's value; e.g., genLab(10) = 'L10'.

Assuming that the inverter has knowledge of the syntax of a label (an 'L' followed by an integer), this production can be inverted as discussed above. This illustrates that additive token permuting functions may be useful inversion technique even in a GRIF

p: if_stmt ::= IF expression THEN statement.
   ‾if_stmt.TRANS = Concatenate(expression.trans,'FJP',
                          genLab(if_stmt.labnum),
         stmt.trans, 'LAB', genLab(if_stmt.labnum));

range(genLab) = label;

Figure 5-6: An additive token permuting function

system allowing multiple trans attributes. As mentioned earlier, the inversion algorithm could make use of a database of productions deriving strings over some common domains (such as the domain of labels). In this case the user need only specify the range of the additive token permuting function and the inversion algorithm would automatically insert the appropriate productions into the inverted grammar.

5.1.2. Deletive token permuting functions

Figure 5-7 presents an AG fragment which mimics the the translation of assignment statements in a Pascal-like language into assignment statements in a C-like language. An assignment statement of the form "f := expression" is translated to "f = expression" when f is a variable and to "return (expression)" when f is the name of the function enclosing the body of this statement[18]. This is implemented by passing the name of the function enclosing the statement into the context of the current production by way of the attribute assnStmt.CUR_FUNC. In this production, Id.value gives the string which Id derives.

q: assnStmt ::= Id := expression.
      assnStmt.trans = if assnStmt.cur_func = Id.value
            then Concatenate('return', '(', expression.trans, ')')
            else Concatenate(Id.trans, '=', expression.trans);

Figure 5-7: A deletive token permuting function

In this production the first part of the token permuting clause is not a token permuting function: it deletes the nonterminal Id. The inverse production corresponding to it

---

[18]This is not an accurate translation from Pascal to C as the function assignment in Pascal can occur many times before function termination whereas the C return statement causes function termination. This example uses a simplified model to illustrate deletive token permuting functions. The examples in appendix B indicate the actual method for correctly translating between Pascal's function assignment and C's return statement.

would have the syntax [qI$_a$: assnStmtI ::= return (expressionI)] and would require its distinguished semantic function to be of the form: <assnStmtI.transinv = Concatenate(IdI.transinv, ':=', expressionI.transinv)>. Of course, this semantic function is not meaningful as it requires the attribute value "IdI.transinv" but Id is not found in the context-free portion of the production.

Once again, it is possible to rewrite this translation as a RIF at the cost of introducing much ambiguity. This could be accomplished by letting the subtree rooted at Id translate either to the name of the Id or to the empty string, depending upon whether the Id is a variable or function name. The details are left to the reader. Instead, note that if a value for IdI.transinv can be synthesized based only upon attributes of the inverted production, then the inversion of the production can be accomplished without introducing extra ambiguity into the specification. Recall that by definition, IdI.transinv gives the string that Id would derive in the original production- which is exactly the value of the attribute Id.value. Using this insight in conjunction with the fact that the condition attached to the first clause of the token permuting clause states that Id.value must equal assnStmt.cur_func, the production q can be inverted to produce the inverse productions given in figure 5-8.

qI$_a$: assnStmtI ::= return (expressionI).
    assnStmt.transinv = Concatenate(assnStmtI.cur_func, ':=',
                expressionI.transinv);

qI$_b$: assnStmtI ::= IdI = expressionI.
    assnStmtI.transinv = if assnStmtI.cur_func = IdI.value
       then ERROR
       else Concatenate(IdI.transinv, ':=', expressionI.transinv);

Figure 5-8: Its inverse

The technique illustrated by this example can be generalized. A function $f(\delta_1, ...,\delta_n)$ is a *deletive token permuting function* over an alphabet Δ if and only if it is of the following form: $f(\delta_1, ...,\delta_n) = $ Concatenate(β_0, δ_{i_1}, β_1, δ_{i_2}, ...,δ_{i_n}, β_n) where each δ_k ($1 \le k \le n$) is in Δ^*, each $i_j \in [1..n]$, $i_j \ne i_k$ for $j \ne k$, and each β_k ($1 \le k \le n$) is a constant in Δ^*. A deletive token permuting function differs from a token permuting function in that not every argument must appear on the right hand side.

In order to make use of deletive token permuting functions, a special synthesized attribute "value" must be associated with each nonterminal. If a nonterminal X has a synthesized attribute X.value, then for any node N labeled X in any semantic tree, N.value = 's' iff N derives 's'. To extend RIF grammars, each primitive clause of a token permuting clause is allowed to be a deletive token permuting function instead of simply a token permuting function if certain conditions are met. For simplicity, the following discussion examines the case where the token permuting clause contains a single token permuting function and where only one argument is deleted by that function; the ideas stated here can be easily generalized by the reader. Let G be a RIF grammar specifying a translation over $\Sigma \times \Delta$ and let $[p: X_0 ::= \alpha_0 X_1 \alpha_1 X_2 \ldots X_{n_p} \alpha_{n_p}]$ be a production in G with the distinguished semantic function corresponding to one of the following two forms:

X_0.trans = if ERROR(X_1.trans, ..., X_{n_p}.trans) or X_j.value $\neq$ g(atts)
    then ERROR
    else f(X_1.trans, ..., X_{n_p}.trans);

X_0.trans = if ERROR(X_1.trans, ..., X_{n_p}.trans) then ERROR
    elsif X_j.value = g(atts)
    then f(X_1.trans, ..., X_{n_p}.trans)
    else ...

where f(X_1.trans, ..., X_{n_p}.trans) = Concatenate(β_0, X_{i_1}.trans,..., X_{n_p}.trans, β_{n_p}) is a deletive token permuting function deleting its argument X_j.trans (i.e., X_j.trans does not appear in the Concatenate function) and atts is a subset of the attributes of the production. Furthermore, assume that

1. no attribute of X_j is used to define any other attribute X_k.att (k $\neq$ j) of the production, with the exception of the above occurrence of of X_j.value in the condition X_j.value $\neq$ g(atts), and

2. for any possible value of g(atts), there exists a valid subtree rooted at X_j such that X_j.value = g(atts).

Then p inverts to $[pI: XI_0 ::= \beta_0 XI_{i_1} \beta_1 \ldots XI_{i_{np}} \beta_{n_p}]$ with the distinguished semantic function

XI_0.trans = if ERROR(XI_{i_1}.transinv,...,$XI_{i_{np}}$.transinv)
    then ERROR

else Concatenate(α_0,XI$_1$.transinv,...,α_{j-1},g(atts),α_{j+1},...,XI$_{n_p}$.transinv,α_{n_p});

Figure 5-9 graphically illustrates the effect of this inversion rule on a production of the form [p: X0 ::= X1 X2 X3] with the distinguished semantic function X0.trans = if X2.value $\neq$ g(atts) then ERROR else Concatenate(X1.trans, X3trans). According to the inversion rule given above, this would invert to [pI: XI0 ::= XI1 XI3] with the distinguished semantic function XI0.transinv = Concatenate(XI1.transinv, g(atts), XI3.transinv). As illustrated by the figure, if the nodes labeled X1, X2, and X3 in the original semantic tree derive the strings s1, s2, and s3 and have translations t1, t2, and t3 respectively, then the node labeled X0 will derive the string s1s2s3 and get translation t1t3. The nodes labeled XI1 and XI3 in the corresponding inverse semantic tree will derive the strings t1 and t3 and get translations s1 and s3 respectively. The node labeled XI0 will derive t1t3 and needs to synthesize the translation s1s2s3, which it can do by substituting the value g(atts) for s2. In order for this to work it must be that no other attributes of X2 are used in the production to define other attributes of X0, X1, or X3. This is because X2 is not in the inverse tree and these attributes will likewise not be in the inverse tree. Secondly, it must be that any value produced by g(atts) could likewise be derived by X2 in some semantic tree. In the INVERT system, a special condition AssertEqual(Xj.trans, g(atts)) is used to specify that

1. Xj.trans = g(atts) and
2. for every possible value of g(atts) = s, there exists some valid semantic tree rooted at Xj deriving s.

When the condition AssertEqual is used in a deletive token permuting function, the inverse production is created as specified above. One problem with the INVERT system should be mentioned. I have found that often a symbol to be deleted has synthesized attributes used in the production, in addition to its trans attribute. When the symbol is deleted these attributes also need to be given a value, but using the current implementation there is no way to do this. A useful improvement to INVERT would be to allow AssertEqual clauses for non-trans attributes of a deleted symbol as well as for the trans attribute.

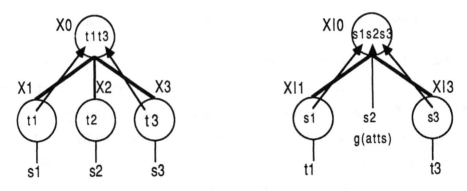

Figure 5-9: Original and inverse trees

Additive token permuting functions and deletive token permuting functions complement one another. Inverting a production whose translation is defined by a deletive token permuting function creates a production whose translation is defined by an additive token permuting function and vice versa. For example, inverting production pI_1 of figure 5-3 will create production p_1 of figure 5-2.

The idea behind deletive token permuting functions could also be adopted into the GRIF paradigm of the previous chapter. GRIFs were formulated so that every node in the original tree contributes at least one trans attribute to the translation. This insures that the original semantic tree can be recovered from the inverse semantic tree. Using the same principle embodied in deletive token permuting functions this restriction can be somewhat relaxed. If it is known that two subtrees of the original semantic tree are identical, then only one of them needs to be represented in the inverse semantic tree. The second subtree can then be obtained from it.

5.2. Invertive token permuting functions

RIFs are good at expressing translations which are inherently string manipulations. However, some translations are best viewed as arithmetic computations, and these are difficult to express using RIFs. For instance, translating x to y, where y equals the square root of x, is best described as an arithmetic operation. Trying to express such computations as RIFs leads to awkward grammars. Put into different terms, RIFs are good at expressing translations in which there exists a similar context-free structure between the input and output strings. But when the translation derived from an input string is not based upon the structure of the parse tree but upon an arbitrary out-of-line semantic function (such as the square root function), then the translation becomes difficult to describe as a RIF.

Most translations, even "string oriented" ones, such as translating between programming languages, often contain aspects of "arithmetic oriented" computations. For example, consider the problem of translating between arrays in C and arrays in Pascal via an intermediate form. A C array declaration such as "int A[5]" must be expressed in Pascal as "A: array [0..4] of integer"[19]. In general, given the C declaration of an array of length J, the Pascal declaration will require the generation of the number K, where K = J - 1. Although there is a simple mathematical correspondence between the numbers J and K, there is no syntactic correspondence between 'J' and 'K', the formal symbols representing these numbers. Hence the translation from C declarations to Pascal declarations is expressed using an out-of-line semantic function shown in figure 5-10. If t is a string representing an integer, then |t| will denote its value. The function Minus(a: integer, s: integerString) returns the string t such that |t| = |s| - a.

arrayDec ::= type Id [integer].
 arrayDec.trans = Concatenate(Id.trans, ': array [0 .. ',
  Minus(1, integer.value), ']', 'of', type.trans);

Figure 5-10: An invertive token permuting function

This example fails to be a RIF since the function computing the trans attribute is not a token permuting function: instead of the argument integer.trans, the function contains

---

[19]In some cases one is able to circumvent the problem of arithmetic operations by treating them as string translations. One might think that in this case one could translate the C array declaration "int A[5]" to the Pascal array declaration "A: array [0..5 - 1] of integer". This is not possible for two reasons. Firstly, Pascal does not allow arithmetic expressions to be used as array bounds. Secondly, if every C declaration of the form "A[Z]" got translated to the Pascal form: "A: array [0..Z - 1]", the inverse AG (translating from Pascal to C) would expect every Pascal program to be of this form. This is not possible, however, as Pascal can have arbitrary array declarations of the form "A: array [Y .. Z]", where Y and Z are arbitrary integers.

the argument Minus(1, integer.value). Let Plus(a: integer, s: integerString) return the string t, where $|t| = |s| + a$. Then Plus(a, s) is the <u>inverse</u> of Minus(a, s). Using this knowledge, the above example can be inverted to produce the production of figure 5-11.

arrayDec ::= Id : array [0 .. integer] of type.
     arrayDec.trans = Concatenate(type.trans, Id.trans, '[',
         Plus(1, integer.value), ']');

Figure 5-11: Its inverse

By supplying to the inversion algorithm knowledge about *inverse semantic functions*, the above sorts of translations can be performed automatically. The following discussion formalizes and generalizes this idea. Let g(a1: t1, ..., ak: tk, B: T) and h(a1: t1, ..., ak: tk, C: T′) be functions such that

   1. the range of h = $T \subseteq \Sigma^*$,

   2. the range of g = $T' \subseteq \Delta^*$, and

   3. g(b1, ..., bk, s) = r iff h(b1, ..., bk, r) = s for all strings r in T′, and s in T.

We then say that g and h are *inverse functions*. We say that a function f is an *invertive token permuting function using g* over an alphabet Δ if and only if it is of the following form: $f(\delta_1, ..., \delta_n; \gamma, a1, a2, ..., ak) = Concatenate(\beta_0, \delta_{i_1}, \beta_1, \delta_{i_2},...,\delta_{i_r}, \beta_r, g(a1, ..., ak, \gamma), \beta_{r+1}, \delta_{i_{r+1}},...,\delta_{i_n}, \beta_{n+1})$ where each δ_k ($1 \leq k \leq n$) is in Δ^*, $[i_1..i_n]$ is a permutation of [1..n], each β_k ($1 \leq k \leq n$) is a constant in Δ^*, g(a1, ..., an, γ) returns a string value in Δ^*, a1, ..., ak are arguments having arbitrary types, and there exists a computable function h such that g and h are inverse functions. Like additive and deletive token permuting functions, invertive token permuting functions are a generalization of token permuting functions.

To extend RIF grammars, each primitive clause of a token permuting clause is allowed to be an invertive token permuting function instead of simply a token permuting function. For simplicity, the following discussion examines the case where the token permuting clause contains a single token permuting function. The ideas stated here can be easily generalized by the reader. Let G be a RIF grammar specifying a translation over $\Sigma \times \Delta$ and let [p: X_0 ::= $\alpha_0 X_1 \alpha_1 X_2 ... X_{n_p} \alpha_{n_p}$] be a production in G with the distinguished semantic function

X_0.trans = if ERROR(X_1.trans, ..., X_{m-1}.trans, X_{m+1}.trans, ..., X_{n_p}.trans)
    then ERROR
    else $f(X_1$.trans, ..., X_{m-1}.trans, X_{m+1}.trans, ..., X_{n_p}.trans; X_m.value, a1, ..., ak)

where f is an invertive token permuting function using g and is of the form:
Concatenate(β_0, X_{i_1}.trans, β_1,...,X_{i_r}.trans, β_r, g(a1, ..., ak, X_m.value), β_{r+1}, $X_{i_{r+1}}$,...,$X_{i_{np}}$.trans, β_{n_p}). X_m.value must give the value of the string derived by X_m and each X_j.trans ($1 \leq j < m$ and $m < j \leq n_p$) must appear exactly once as some X_{i_k}.trans. Notice that n_p-1 right-part symbols of the production contribute a trans attribute to f and that the remaining right-part symbol (X_m) contributes a value attribute. (Recall that the value attribute gives the string derived from a nonterminal in a parse tree and the trans attribute gives the translation of the subtree beneath the nonterminal). Let g and h be inverse functions with the range of g = T′. Let Q be a context-free symbol deriving strings over the domain of T′ with one synthesized attribute Q.value. Then p inverts to [pI: XI_0 ::= β_0 XI_{i_1} β_1 ... XI_{i_r} β_r Q β_{r+1} ... $XI_{i_{np}}$ β_{n_p}] with the distinguished semantic function

XI_0.trans = if ERROR(XI_{i_1}.transinv,..., $XI_{i_{np}}$.transinv)
    then ERROR
    else Concatenate(α_0, XI_1.transinv, ..., XI_{m-1}.transinv, α_{m-1},
        h(a1, ..., ak, Q.value), α_{m+1}, XI_{m+1}, ..., XI_{n_p}.transinv, α_{n_p});

The basic idea behind this inversion technique is as follows: in the original production, X_m derives some string s. This string is given in the attribute X_m.value. The function g uses the value of s, along with any other needed information, to generate a translation r. The goal in inverting the production is to perform the inverse operation- to generate the translation s from the input string r. Since h is the inverse of function g, this can be performed quite simply. By passing r as an argument to h, the string s will be produced. The nonterminal Q is only introduced to generate strings over the range of g. If it happens that f and g have the same range then no new nonterminal Q needs to be introduced. The same nonterminal X_m used in the original production can also be used in the inverse production. This is usually the case for arithmetic operations, as illustrated by figures 5-10 and 5-11. In that example both functions Minus and Plus are of type integer.

By slightly relaxing the definition of inverse functions, they can be very useful to express even more translations. In particular, say that the AG G translates all strings in T′ to the same string r. The inverse grammar G^{-1} needs to translate r back to <u>some</u> string in T′- but it does not matter which one. Along these lines the definition of inverse functions can be relaxed so that if g is a many-to-one translation used in a token permuting function, its inverse function h can still be one-to-one. The example of figure 5-12 illustrates this idea. The production p derives the syntax of a Pascal program heading. This syntax indicates that a Pascal program heading consists of the keyword "program" followed by the program name followed by input and output parameters (for simplicity we assume that the only program parameters are input and output parameters). No matter what the name of the Pascal program is, the name of the translated C program must be "main", since all C programs have a main routine of that name. Hence the function VarToMain translates the Pascal program name to the standard name "main". The inverse function of VarToMain is MainToVar and it translates back from the C standard program name "main" to an arbitrary Pascal program name (in actuality, it is implemented as the identity function translating "main" to "main"). The generated inverse production pI is also given in that figure.

```
p: programHeading ::= PROGRAM Id ( inputAndOutput ) ;
      programHeading.trans = Concatenate(VarToMain(Id.value),
                   inputAndOutput.trans);

inverse(VarToMain) = MainToVar;
--------------------------------------------------------------------------------
pI: programHeadingI ::= IdI inputAndOutputI.
      programHeadingI.transinv = Concatenate("PROGRAM",
        MainToVar(IdI.value), "(", inputAndOutputI.transinv, ")");
```

Figure 5-12: Less restricted inverse functions

Invertive token permuting functions were primarily formulated for expressing arithmetic operations so that they could be inverted. To this end, the inversion algorithm could be built to contain knowledge about common arithmetic operations and their inverses, such as addition/subtraction, multiplication/division, and exponentiation/taking the nth root. If more complicated functions are required they can either be built up out of these primitives or they can be supplied as input into the inversion algorithm as a supplement to the RIF grammar. This latter method is used in INVERT. For each pair of inverse functions f and g used in the grammar, a definition of the form "inverse(f) = g" is required. The current implementation of INVERT requires that all inverse pairs of functions have the same type. A different approach to inverting semantic functions is to express them in a restricted logic programming paradigm that is bi-directional. This approach needs more research (see [55]). The approach used here, based on invertive token permuting functions, is similar to the approach advocated in [54], where the Prolog interpreter is equipped with knowledge on how to invert specific Prolog constructs, such as mathematical functions.

5.3. Mechanisms for dealing with ambiguity

In section 3.3 we saw that an inverted grammar may be ambiguous even if the original grammar is unambiguous or even LR(0). My experience shows that this is not just a theoretical result but that the inverted grammar often contains some ambiguity or non-LALR constructs. Section 7.1 will discuss a general paradigm for building a translator based upon ambiguous AGs. Unfortunately, the AG evaluator I am currently using (Linguist [19]) interfaces with a standard shift/reduce parser (YACC [33]) and assumes that only one parse exists. Therefore any ambiguity in the inverse AG will be arbitrarily resolved, perhaps incorrectly. To overcome this problem, INVERT incorporates two mechanisms for removing ambiguity from the inverse grammar.

One simple form of ambiguity that is often present in an inverted attribute grammar is where the context-free portion of several productions are the same but have different semantics. For example, consider the productions of figure 5-13 and the inverse productions of figure 5-14.

This example presents three (simplified) productions from an AG translating C to ABSIM, an intermediate form discussed in chapter 6. Like Pascal, ABSIM only allows direct references to an identifier; no pointer arithmetic is allowed. When translating

p1: primaryP1Exp ::= Id.
   primaryP1Exp.trans = if primaryP1Exp.expected_vv_type <>
       lookUpValOrVarType(Id.ntx, primaryP1Exp.symtab_in)
      then ERROR
      else Id.trans,
  (... other semantics ...)

p2: primaryP1Exp ::= * Id.
   primaryP1Exp.trans =
    if not(primaryP1Exp.expected_vv_type = valType and
       lookUpValOrVarType(Id.ntx, primaryP1Exp.symtab_in) = varType)
      then ERROR
      else Id.trans,
  (... other semantics ...)

p3: primaryP1Exp ::= & Id.
   primaryP1Exp.trans = if not(primaryP1Exp.expected_vv_type = varType and
   lookUpValOrVarType(Id.ntx, primaryP1Exp.symtab_in) = valType)
      then ERROR
      else Id.trans;
  (... other semantics ...)

Figure 5-13: Productions from the C-to-Pascal translator

from C to ABSIM, any C pointer arithmetic must be translated into non-pointer arithmetic if this can be done. If a parameter to a C function is a pointer to an identifier, then the corresponding ABSIM function can pass that identifier as a variable (''var'') argument. The AG translating from C to ABSIM enters each identifier into the symbol table as either valType or varType, depending upon whether the C function declares the identifier as a regular identifier or as a pointer. For instance, the declaration ''int a, *b;'' would cause a to be assigned valType and b to be assigned varType. Any reference to an identifier in the C program, whether of the form 'V', '*V', or '&V', will be translated to the ABSIM code 'V'. Nonetheless, the translation must first be checked to be legal; e.g., given the C expression '*V', it must be checked that V is of type varType and that the expected value of the expression is of type valType. Hence ''Y = *V'' would be translated to ''Y := V'' as long as Y is of type valType and V is of type varType but would produce ERROR otherwise. Similarly ''Y = &V'' would be translated to ''Y := V'' if Y is of type varType and V is of type valType. The inverse productions given in figure 5-14 all have different semantics but the same context-free portion. They indicate that when translating the intermediate form back to C, a variable such as 'V' should be

pI1:primaryP1ExpI ::= IdI.
  primaryP1ExpI.transinv = if primaryP1ExpI.expected_vv_type <>
          lookUpValOrVarType(IdI.ntx, primaryP1ExpI.symtab_in)
    then ERROR
    else IdI.transinv,
  (... other semantics ...)

pI2: primaryP1ExpI ::= IdI.
  primaryP1ExpI.transinv =
    if not (primaryP1ExpI.expected_vv_type = valType and
      lookUpValOrVarType(IdI.ntx, primaryP1ExpI.symtab_in) = varType)
    then ERROR
    else Concatenate("*", IdI.transinv),
  (... other semantics ...)

pI3: primaryP1ExpI ::= IdI.
  primaryP1ExpI.transinv =
    if not (primaryP1ExpI.expected_vv_type = varType and
      lookUpValOrVarType(IdI.ntx, primaryP1ExpI.symtab_in) = valType)
    then ERROR
    else Concatenate("&", IdI.transinv),
  (... other semantics ...)

Figure 5-14: Productions with the same context-free portion

translated to either 'V', '*V', or '&V', depending upon the context. Since the context-free portion of these productions is the same, the syntax alone is not enough to determine which production to apply. Ideally, the correct parse would be found by evaluating the semantics of each production and choosing one which has a non-ERROR translation. Unfortunately, before evaluating any semantics, a typical shift/reduce parser would arbitrarily choose one of these productions to apply, perhaps the wrong one.

A solution to this problem is *collapsing productions*. The basic idea is to take all the productions with the same context-free portion and to create a single production from them. For example, the three productions of figure 5-14 would all be collapsed to the single production of figure 5-15.[20]

Let p1 and p2 be two productions with the same context-free portion, $[X_0 ::= \alpha_0 X_1 \alpha_1 X_2 ... X_{n_p} \alpha_{n_p}]$. Let p1 have a distinguished semantic function of the

---

[20]In this figure, we use the notation "<name> : <type> = <value>" to express that the temporary attribute called "name", of the given type, has value given by <value>. This is merely a device used in the Linguist system to avoid redundant computations.

pI1:primaryP1ExpI ::= IdI.
  C1: boolean = primaryP1ExpI.expected_vv_type <>
          lookUpValOrVarType(IdI.ntx, primaryP1ExpI.symtab_in),
  C2: boolean = not (primaryP1ExpI.expected_vv_type = valType and
    lookUpValOrVarType(IdI.ntx, primaryP1ExpI.symtab_in) = varType),
  C3: boolean = not (primaryP1ExpI.expected_vv_type = varType and
    lookUpValOrVarType(IdI.ntx, primaryP1ExpI.symtab_in) = valType),
  primaryP1ExpI.transinv = if C1 and C2 and C3
    then ERROR
    elsif not(C1) then IdI.transinv
    elsif not(C2) then Concatenate("*", IdI.transinv)
    else Concatenate("&", IdI.transinv),
(... other semantics ...)

Figure 5-15: The collapsed production

form: $<X_0.trans =$ if C1 then ERROR else $f(X_1.trans, ..., X_{n_p}.trans)>$ and let p2 have the distinguished semantic function of the form: $<X_0.trans =$ if C2 then ERROR else $g(X_1.trans, ..., X_{n_p}.trans)>$. Assuming that the clauses C1 and C2 are <u>mutually exclusive</u>, an equivalent grammar can be created by collapsing the two productions to form a new production p. The context-free portion of p is the same as p1 and p2. The distinguished semantic function of p is of the form $<X_0.trans =$ if C1 and C2 then ERROR elsif not(C1) then $f(X_1.trans, ..., X_{n_p}.trans)$ else $g(X_1.trans, ..., X_{n_p}.trans)>$. Furthermore, if the attribute $X_i.att$ is defined by a function h in p1 and by a different function k in p2, then in p it is defined by the function: $<X_i.att =$ if not(C1) then h else k>.[21] Collapsing productions is easily extended to deal with a set of context-free productions $\{p1, ..., pn\}$, all with the same context-free portion. As an exercise, the reader may wish to use this algorithm to collapse productions pI_1 and pI_2 of example 3-2 into a single production.

As mentioned above, one can only guarantee that collapsing two productions together will result in an equivalent grammar if the boolean clauses C1 and C2 are mutually exclusive. If they are not mutually exclusive, then there may be some context in which

---

[21]This process can create extra semantic dependencies in the inverted AG. For example, if C1 references an attribute $X_i.b$, then in the collapsed production there will be a dependency from $X_i.b$ to $X_i.att$, even though no such dependency existed in either non-collapsed production. In one of my inverted AGs, such extra semantic dependencies actually caused the generated evaluator to require an additional pass.

both C1 and C2 are valid, but only the application of production p2 will result in a valid semantic tree. Since the way production p is constructed results in choosing production p1 before p2, a non-valid semantic tree may possibly be built.

In the INVERT system, after an AG is inverted it is fed into a postprocessor called COLLAPSE. This program takes the inverted AG and produces a collapsed AG, using the algorithm outlined above. Since the problem of determining whether or not two boolean clauses compute mutually exclusive predicates is not solvable, the program assumes that all of the boolean clauses are mutually exclusive. My experience shows that in practical settings this is almost always the case, and that even when it is not the case, it makes no difference which production is chosen; i.e., both will result in valid semantic trees. COLLAPSE also produces a documentation file which lists all collapsed productions, so that any mistakes in this matter can be checked by the user.

Although collapsing productions can only be appled in limited circumstances, it has been quite useful in practice. In the INVERT-generated ABSIM-to-C AG, 17 out of 208 productions were collapsed. It would be interesting to investigate ways of extending COLLAPSE, so that it could statically detect and remove ambiguity from the grammar spread out over several productions. (Although the problem is not solvable in general, there may several practical heuristics for identifying ambiguity in limited situations.)

Even with COLLAPSE, several of my grammars still retained some ambiguity. This was usually due to the fact that the original grammar specified a many-to-one translation. Since the inverted grammar specified a one-to-many grammar, an input string could be parsed in more than one way. In order to rid the grammar of this ambiguity, the INVERT system allows the RIF writer to specify that a production (or part of a production) is not to be inverted. Consider the problem of translating C for-loops to Pascal (via the intermediate form ABSIM). Some C for-loops can be translated to Pascal for-loops but some need to be translated to Pascal while-loops. A C loop such as "for (i = e1; i $\leq$ e2; i ++) stat" can be translated to the Pascal for-loop "for i = e1 to e2 do stat". A C loop such as "for (i = e1; z $\geq$ e2; e3) stat", on the other hand, needs to be translated to the Pascal code "i := e1; while z ≥ e2 do begin stat; evaluateBool(e3) end". The production of figure 5-16 gives a simplified version of the production of my C-to-ABSIM AG that accomplishes this task. The temporary boolean attribute GEN_FOR indicates whether an ABSIM for-loop (which closely resembles the syntax of the C for-loop) or an ABSIM while-loop should be generated. If the subtree rooted at an fexpr is of the form: "i = expression" then fexpr.for1 will equal the symbol table index number of the variable i, otherwise it will equal the null index (nullNtx). Similarly, if the subtree rooted at an fexpr is of the form: "i ≤ expression" (or a variant) then fexpr.for2 will equal the symbol table index number of the variable i, otherwise it will equal the null index. Finally, if the subtree rooted at an fexpr is of the form: "i++" (or a variant) then fexpr.for3 will equal the symbol table index number of the variable i, otherwise it will equal the null index. If fexpr1.for1 = fexpr2.for2 = fexpr3.for3 <> nullNtx then this C loop can be translated in a straightforward fashion to a Pascal loop and hence an ABSIM for-loop is generated. Otherwise an ABSIM while loop is generated. The information concerning whether a for-loop or while-loop is generated is passed back down the tree (via fexpr.for_gen) in order for the subtrees to generate the appropriate translation.

In this example, the token permuting function generating a while loop is prefaced by the keyword "*NOGEN". This tells INVERT not to generate an inverse production for this token permuting function. This is because there already exists an inverse production to recognize while loops in ABSIM (the production that generates ABSIM while-loops from C while loops inverts to recognize ABSIM while-loops and generate C while-loops). Hence if an inverse production was generated for this token permuting function extra ambiguity would be introduced into the ABSIM-to-C AG.

This method for removing ambiguity is used in several places in my grammars, and turns out to be quite useful in practice. Nonetheless, it is a somewhat dangerous technique. By giving the user the power to remove productions from the inverted grammar, one can no longer guarantee that the generated grammar is truly the inverse of

```
forStmt ::= FOR ( fexpr1 ; fexpr2 ; fexpr3 ) statement.
    GEN_FOR:boolean = (fexpr1.for1 = fexpr2.for2) and
                (fexpr1.for1 = fexpr3.for3) and
                (fexpr1.for1 <> nullNtx),
    forStmt.trans = if GEN_FOR
        then Concatenate("FŌR", fexpr1.trans, ";", fexpr2.trans, ";",
            fexpr3.trans,"DO", statement.trans)
        else *NOGEN Concatenate(fexpr1.trans, "WHILE", fexpr2.trans, "DO",
            "BEGIN", statement.trans, fexpr3.trans, "END")
        endif,
    fexpr1.for_gen = GEN_FOR,
    fexpr2.for_gen = GEN_FOR,
    fexpr3.for_gen = GEN_FOR,
    (...other semantics...)
```

Figure 5-16:   Translating C for-loops

the original one.   Ideally, the user would only remove productions which are superfluous- if there exists a valid semantic tree for some input using a production which is to be removed then there will exist another valid semantic tree for that input without using that production.   Unfortunately, it may be that the user removes a production which is not "covered" by any other production in the grammar.

5.4. Summary

This chapter discussed INVERT.   The goal of this software is to provide a <u>flexible</u> bi-directional translator-writing system.   For this reason, many extensions to the basic inversion paradigm are included in INVERT.   Although some of these extensions are similar to the generalized RIFs of the last chapter, unlike GRIFs, the INVERT system produces AGs that can be run in traditional AG-based environments.   Furthermore, INVERT was built to support translations that occur in practice.   It therefore includes facilities to handle numeric oriented computations, many-to-one translations, etc. Whereas GRIFs were formulated as a natural generalization of RIFs, expressing interesting theoretical characteristics, INVERT was formulated as a practical system to be used in conjunction with existing AG-based translator-writing systems.

In chapter 1, we stated that AG inversion could be used to build source-to-source translators.   Having built INVERT, we could now proceed to test this proposition.   The next chapter details our methodology and then describes the source-to-source translators we produced using INVERT.

Chapter 6

Translating between programming languages

Automatic translation between programming languages is an important tool for increasing program reusability. Often the need arises to transport a large software system from one source language environment to another. Performing such a translation by hand is a large undertaking, costly in manpower and very error-prone. For this reason, several researchers have built automated tools to aid them in particular such projects [13, 1].

Obviously, when translating from one programming language to another, it must be guaranteed that the produced program is semantically equivalent to the original one. Less obvious but equally important is that the produced program have a structure similar to the original one. Preserving program structure is important in order to insure code readability, maintainability, and efficiency [41]. This is because the structure imposed upon a program by the designer implicitly encodes a computation model. By preserving program structure one is able to preserve this model, and therefore aid the reader to more easily understand design decisions and aid the compiler to optimize the code.

This chapter presents a methodology for building source-to-source translators, based upon AG inversion. The basic idea behind this methodology is to (i) construct a canonical form in which programs of all source languages can be represented and (ii) write invertible AGs from each source language into this canonical form. Then, using the inversion algorithm outlined in this thesis, one can automatically obtain the inverse translators, translating from the canonical form back to each programming language. By composing the appropriate pairs of translators thus obtained, one can create a source-to-source translator between any pair of languages. This method is illustrated by the diagram of figure 6-1. Although it depicts the construction for four languages, the construction is equally valid for two or for one hundred languages. Using an intermediate language, one can produce n^2 source-to-source translators from only $2n$ AG specifications. Using AG inversion, the n^2 translators can be produced from only n AG specifications! We call the method outlined here the *inversion approach* to source-to-source translation.

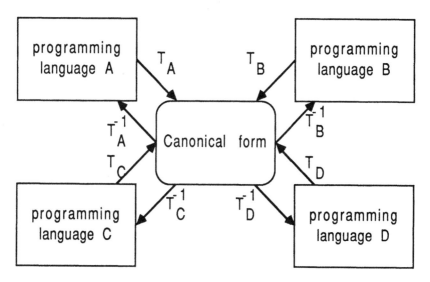

Figure 6-1: Source-to-source translation using AG inversion

This diagram is somewhat misleading, as in a real system, invertible translators would only be one portion of the entire system. Other modules, preprocessors and postprocessors, would also be needed to massage the text into appropriate formats, or even to perform parts of the translation that are difficult to perform in invertible translators. Furthermore, the translated program will often need to make use of routines from a run-time library built by the translator writer. Because this thesis is primarily concerned with the role of AG inversion in the translation process, we will ignore these other aspects of translators for the most part. However, in section 6.3, when discussing our Pascal and C translators, these other modules will once again make their appearance.

The inversion approach to source-to-source translation has many benefits. The use of a canonical representation provides a useful factorization of the translation problem. Secondly, by concentrating on a common representation in which to represent program constructs, one is forced to identify the trouble spots where the languages are incompatible early in the development cycle. Thirdly, by automatically inverting the AGs, more of the software burden is placed on the computer and less on the user. Most importantly, the use of inversion guarantees that the inverted AG is the actual inverse of the original.

The success of the inversion approach to source-to-source translation hinges upon (i) ones ability to find an adequate canonical form and (ii) ones ability to write invertible AGs from each programming language into this canonical form. The preceding chapters of this thesis have focused on the latter topic and demonstrated how invertible AGs can be written to express complex translations. One of the goals of this chapter is to examine the issues involved in choosing the right canonical form. As we shall see, a careful analysis of the source languages is warranted before a particular canonical form is adopted. The time spent designing the canonical form will be more then compensated for later on in the project.

In order to prove the feasibility of the inversion approach to source-to-source translation, I have constructed source-to-source translators for the Pascal and C programming languages. This was done by formulating a canonical representation in which most Pascal and C constructs can be expressed and then writing invertible AGs from the source languages into this canonical form. These AGs were automatically inverted using the INVERT system, described in chapter 5.

This chapter ties together the idea of AG inversion and source-to-source translation. It also shows describes the Pascal-to-C and C-to-Pascal translators which have been built using this approach. Section 6.1 focusses on a general approach to choosing a good canonical form and section 6.2 discusses the canonical form used for the Pascal-to-C and C-to-Pascal translators. In particular, it will discuss some of the differences between these source languages and how it influenced the choice of the canonical form. In section 6.3 an overview of the translators is presented and section 6.4 describes a preprocessor used to "denest" Pascal procedures.

The philosophy we adopt concerning source-to-source translation is that it is essential to preserve program structure when translating between languages. Without preserving program structure, the translated program will not be readable, nor maintainable. Often it will be very inefficient. Maintaining program structure, however, is only possible if there are constructs in each language to model constructs in the other language (such constructs are called *portable* in [41]). Consider, for example, the languages C and Pascal. Both are Turing equivalent, and it is therefore possible to construct a semantically equivalent Pascal program for any C program and vice versa. In practice, however, there is no good way of describing a C program containing complex pointer arithmetic in Pascal. Therefore our C-to-Pascal translator does not handle complex C pointer arithmetic. This is not related to the inversion approach to source-to-source translation but to the inherent difference in expressibilty between the languages. Should one devise some scheme to translate complex C pointer arithmetic into Pascal, it could be performed in an invertible translator.

6.1. Constructing a greatest common divisor canonical form

As described above, the inversion approach to source-to-source translation requires an *adequate* canonical form to represent all source language programs. The canonical form is termed *adequate* iff it meets the following criteria:

1. Every program (in <u>each</u> source language) must be expressible as a program in the canonical form, and

2. every canonical form program that is the image of one translation must be expressible as the image of every other translation.

One can express these criteria as properties of the translation specifications instead of properties of the canonical form: each AG T_i must map the programs of language L_i <u>onto</u> the canonical form. If this is the case, then the inverse AG T_i^{-1} will map every canonical form program back to a program of language L_i.

In order to insure that the canonical form is adequate, one might believe that it should contain only very low level constructs, such as assignment and goto statements, as found in many intermediate codes used in compilers. The logic behind this thinking is best explained by an example. Suppose that language A contains high level flow control constructs, such as for-loops, but that language B does not. If the canonical form contains for-loops then a problem will exist when translating from the canonical form back to language B. Since no program in language B would be mapped to a canonical form representation containing for-loops, the inverse translator for language B would not recognize for-loops in the canonical form. I.e., since T_B is not onto, T_B^{-1} will not define translations on all canonical form programs. This example suggests that to insure the adequacy of the canonical form, it must be composed of only very low level constructs. A closer examination of the problem, however, reveals strong reasons for including high level constructs in the canonical form.

Firstly, if the canonical form is very low level, it is hard to retain program structure when translating from source to source. Translating from the original program into the canonical form will essentially be the same as compiling, whereas translating from the canonical form to the target program will be similar to decompiling [68]. In the end, there is little likelihood that the two programs will share much in common, even though they will be semantically equivalent. As mentioned earlier, preserving program structure is important to insure code readability, maintainability, and efficiency. By making the canonical form too low level, we are throwing away more information than we need to.

Another reason not to make the canonical form a low level language concerns the efficiency of the translators that will be generated. Let T_A be the AG translating the language A into the canonical form and T_A^{-1} its inverse. If the canonical form is very low level, then the translation T_A will be many-to-one in the extreme. For example, if the canonical form doesn't contain any iterative loop structure but uses gotos instead, then one will not be able to tell, looking at a canonical form program containing gotos, whether the original program used gotos or for-loops. In terms of the inverse AG, this means that T_A^{-1} will have a very ambiguous context-free grammar. For a given canonical form program, there may be many parses, each producing different translations. Since each parse may be found to be syntactically or semantically invalid as more of the program is parsed and the semantic tree is evaluated, this introduces much inefficiency in the generated translators. Hence preserving structures of the original program is not only important for its own sake, but is also important for efficiency reasons.

Instead of minimalizing the canonical representation, we want it to serve as the *greatest common divisor* between the languages (in the terminology of [41], we place a *maximality requirement* on the canonical form). As an example, consider the for-loops of Pascal and the for-loops of C. Every for-loop in Pascal has a C for-loop counterpart but the converse is not true. Because we want to maintain program structure as much as possible, our intermediate representation takes the greatest common divisor between the two; in this case, it would include, up to syntactic isomorphism, the Pascal for-loop. Note that this will place a greater burden on our translators. Instead of blindly translating C for-loops into lower level constructs, it must now distinguish whether or not the C for-loop qualifies as a canonical form for-loop. If so, it translates it to that construct; otherwise it has no choice but to replace the for-loop by some other compatible structure (such as a while-loop).

In summary, a careful design of the canonical form is warranted. In deciding the appropriate level of granularity of the canonical form, conflicting goals must be resolved. On one hand, the fact that all source language programs must be representable in the canonical form calls for using low level constructs. On the other hand, the desirability of a canonical form which preserves program structure encourages the use of high level constructs. The resolution of these conflicting goals is found by designing the canonical form to reflect the greatest common divisor (GCD) between the source languages. The granularity of this canonical form is fine enough to represent all source language programs but coarse enough to preserve as much program structure as possible.

Using a greatest common divisor canonical form, every canonical form program will have a source language counterpart.

If the canonical form greatly resembles the source languages (we have a "large" GCD), then we will be able to produce high quality translators which are capable of preserving much program structure. If, however, the canonical form does not closely resemble the source languages (it is a "small" GCD), then the produced translators will not be able to do a good job in preserving program structure. This leads to an important observation regarding source-to-source translation: there is no one good canonical form for representing programs of all programming languages. To the contrary, the inversion approach to source-to-source translation calls for customizing the canonical form to reflect the greatest common divisor of the source languages involved. By considering just a few related languages, we can produce a canonical form closely resembling the source languages. But as we consider more and more languages, each very different from the other, the canonical form becomes reduced to an extremely low level language and the source-to-source translators will not produce high quality translations.

In contrast to the inversion approach to source-to-source translation, many previous endeavors sought extremely general techniques for porting software, sometimes based upon the idea of a universal intermediate language[22]. They hoped that this intermediate language would serve as a canonical form in which to represent programs of all programming languages. Needless to say, these efforts were, in retrospect, overly ambitious. The methodology advocated in [3, 41], on the other hand, is very similar to the inversion approach to source-to-source translation. Their work focuses on two particular languages, Pascal and Ada. They define subsets of these languages, PascalA and AdaP, that are isomorphic to one another. Pascal-to-Ada (or Ada-to-Pascal) translation then becomes a two stage task: first translating from Pascal to PascalA and then translating from PascalA to AdaP. The use of isomorphic sublanguages is

---

[22]The idea of a universal intermediate language, UNCOL, can be found in [57]. For an overview of some early attempts at source-to-source translation, see [11].

comparable to the use of a GCD canonical form. Similar to our preceding discussion on what the canonical form should look like, [41] contains a discussion concerning what portion of the original languages should be contained in the isomorphic sublanguages. The work described in [10] also uses the isomorphic sublanguage approach for implementing a Euclid to Ada translator.

The inversion approach to source-to-source translation formulated here advocates writing AGs translating each source language into the canonical form and using inversion to generate the translators from the canonical form back to each source language. An alternative is to originally write AGs translating from the canonical form into each source language and to then generate inverse AGs translating each source language back to the canonical form. One of the advantages of this approach is that is allows for a *least common multiple* (instead of a GCD) canonical form. This approach has other drawbacks, however. The strengths and weaknesses of the method will be discussed in section 7.2.

6.2. ABSIM: a canonical form for Pascal and C

The previous section detailed a method for building a source-to-source translator based on a canonical representation and AG inversion. It is not hard to see that the method will work well if all the languages are closely related to one another. In such a case it is fairly obvious what the canonical form should look like, and the invertible RIFs of chapter 2 are adequate to express the translations into this canonical form. Hence this strategy can be used to build translators between dialects of a programming language or between closely related formats for representing processed manuscripts [49].

In order to show that this technique could also be used to express more complex translations, I decided to apply the methodology to build translators between the Pascal and C programming languages. This research was interesting for two reasons. Firstly, by attempting to phrase the translations as RIF grammars, I became aware of the need to generalize the RIF formalism. The results of this endeavor have already been discussed in chapters 4 and 5. Secondly, this project helped to clarify the issues involved in choosing a proper intermediate form.

For my Pascal and C translators, I at first chose a widely-known intermediate representation used for compilers (a variant of Ucode). As explained in the last section, I soon discovered the pitfalls of this choice and realized the importance of a GCD canonical form. This led me to closely analyze the two languages and to create a canonical form, called ABSIM, which reflects the greatest common divisor between Pascal and C. It omits any idiosyncrasy peculiar to only one of the languages, while reflecting, as much as possible, the structure common to both languages. For example, Pascal and C have different conventions on returning function values. Whereas C uses a ''return'' statement, Pascal uses function assignment. The C convention provides an implicit transfer of control to the end of the function whereas the Pascal convention provides an implicit temporary variable. ABSIM, being a common denominator between the languages, has neither of these capabilities. Therefore, when translating a C function into the canonical form, the implicit transfer of control of the return statement must be made explicit (using a goto). Similarly, the implicit temporary variable supplied by the function name in Pascal programs must be allocated explicitly in the canonical form.

In designing the GCD canonical form, it is useful to compare the languages to one another and write down a list of those areas where the languages diverge. Using such a list one can deduce those constructs common to both languages and thereby develop the GCD canonical form. To illustrate this process, the rest of this section lists some of the differences between Pascal and C. This list is not intended to be inclusive nor to serve as a comparative study of the languages. (For a comparison of Pascal and C, see [22] and [28]). Those parts of the language which are not included in the language subsets implemented by the Pascal-to-C and C-to-Pascal translators are not discussed at all. This list was compiled when developing ABSIM and is reproduced below in order to demonstrate the type of language comparison needed to form a GCD canonical form. It also documents the subsets of the Pascal and C that have been implemented in the translators. The comparison is based on the C and Pascal reference manuals [27, 32, 35].

1. <u>Syntactic differences</u>. The vast majority of differences between Pascal and C are syntactic differences. Although these are usually straightforward to deal with, they sometimes contain subtleties requiring careful treatment. For example, Pascal and C differ in their use of semicolons and block delimiters, and some analysis is needed to translate these constructs properly. C also contains many shorthand conventions (such as ++, +=, etc.) which need to be expanded into their Pascal counterparts. (See example 4, for instance, in appendix B).

2. <u>Parameter passing conventions</u>. In C there is no call by reference (variable parameters) as there is in Pascal. To achieve the same goal, one must use pointer parameters in C. Different addressing modes must be introduced into the translated C program to deal with these new parameter conventions. (See examples 5 and 7 in appendix B).

3. <u>Control flow</u>. In C, the return statement is used not only to indicate the value that the function will return, but also to terminate function execution. As there is no equivalent statement in Pascal, termination of the function must be obtained by using other control flow constructs, such as a goto statement or a while-loop. This will also cause the introduction of auxiliary goto labels or loop control variables into the Pascal program. The C break statement is dealt with analogously. (See example 1 in appendix B).

4. <u>Function assignment</u>. In Pascal, the name of the function can be used as a temporary variable, which is not the case in C. Therefore, the equivalent C function must be supplied with a temporary variable (whose type corresponds to the function type), and the final value of this variable must be the value returned by the function. (See examples 6, 7, and 8 in appendix B).

5. Assignments within expressions. In C, an assignment can be found within an expression. This cannot be done in Pascal. Auxiliary functions must be provided in the translated Pascal program to mimic the C assignment expressions by Pascal function calls. For example, the C statement "while ((c = getchar()) != 'a')" would be translated in Pascal to "while (assignChar(c, getchar()) <> 'a')", where assignChar(var ch: char; exp: char) is a function which assigns the value exp to ch and returns the value of exp. The assignChar function would be included in the Pascal translation library.

6. Array conventions. In Pascal arrays can have arbitrary lower bounds whereas in C all arrays begin at 0. This means that a Pascal program containing an array not beginning at 0 must be translated to the equivalent C program with the array beginning at 0. All array references must be translated appropriately. (See examples 6 and 7 in appendix B).

7. Int and char types. In C, there is a free intermingling between integer and character types, whereas in Pascal these are looked upon as two distinct types. If a C construct employs implicit conversion between these types, the conversion must be made explicit in the translated Pascal program. For example, the C statements "char ch, chh; chh = (ch - 'a')" must be translated to the Pascal statements "var ch, chh : char; chh := chr(ord(ch) - ord('a'))". (See examples 1 and 2 in appendix B).

8. Boolean expressions. In C there is no boolean type; "boolean" expressions (such as exp in "if exp then ...") do not return a boolean value, but an integer value (0 or 1). In Pascal, the type boolean is an abstract data type, distinct from the type integer. A Pascal program containing boolean definitions must be translated appropriately. Furthermore, if a C program intermingles the value of boolean and integer expressions, this implicit conversion must be made explicit in the Pascal program. For example, the C statements "int a, b, c; while (a = (b || c < 10)) ..." would be translated to the Pascal statements "var a, b, c: integer; while intToBool(assignInt(a, boolToInt(intToBool(b) or c < 10))) ...", where intToBool and boolToInt are library routines performing the expected conversions. (See example 3 in appendix B).

9. _I/O routines_. In Pascal, I/O operations are part of the language definition whereas in C they are system function calls. In practice C provides much greater flexibility in I/O operations. Although all C I/O operations could be mimicked by Pascal functions, I have only implemented the most commonly used C I/O functions (such as scanf, printf, getchar, etc.) where there is a fairly straightforward translation into Pascal I/O primitives. (See examples 1, 5, 6 and 7 in appendix B). More complex I/O operations would need to make use of Pascal library routines.

10. _Addressing modes_. C allows for pointer arithmetic whereas Pascal does not. Although in general there is no any good way to translate C programs using arbitrary pointer arithmetic, restricted uses of pointer arithmetic have a straightforward counterpart in Pascal. For example, call by reference is mimicked in C by passing a pointer to the object. The C-to-Pascal translator can usually replace such pointer arithmetic using "var" parameters. (See examples 2 and 3 in appendix B). Similarly, pointer arithmetic in C used to reference array addresses can often be imitated in Pascal by introducing a new variable. This variable is initialized to the lower bounds of the array (in C, this is always 0) and is incremented whenever the pointer to the array is incremented. For example, the C function

```
void f(a) int a[10]; {
     a++;
     *a = 5;}
```

can be translated to the Pascal procedure

```
procedure f(var a: array [0..9] of integer);
var aIndex: integer;
begin
     aIndex := 0;
     aIndex := aIndex + 1;
     a[aIndex] := 5
end;
```

This translation can only be performed if all invocations of f are passed a pointer to the beginning of the array.

11. _Scoping_. C allows for nested declarations; variables can be declared within blocks. In Pascal, only top level declarations, global to the program or function, are allowed.

When translating a C program to a Pascal program, the inner C declarations must be moved to the top of the function. Name conflicts must be resolved. (See example 2 in appendix B).

12. Initializers. C allows for the declaration of a variable to contain an initializer, giving the value that the variable is to have at the beginning of its lifetime. In Pascal this is not allowed. Such C initializers must be moved to the beginning of the executable statements in the equivalent Pascal program. (See examples 2 and 4 in appendix B).

13. Nested procedures. Pascal allows for procedures (functions) to be built locally within other procedures (and functions). As C does not allow these constructs, all nested Pascal programs must be "denested". This denesting process must maintain the proper run-time environment. The denesting algorithm will be presented in section 6.4. It has been implemented as a separate preprocessing stage of the Pascal-to-C translator (and not included in the main invertible translators). The reason for this is also discussed in section 6.4. (Also see examples 7 and 8 in appendix B).

14. Operator precedence. Pascal and C assign different precedence to equivalent operators. For example, because C assigns a higher precedence to "<" than to "==", the C expression "6 < 7 == 4 < 5" is semantically equivalent to "(6 < 7) == (4 < 5)". Pascal, on the other hand, assigns the same precedence to "=" as to "<". Therefore the Pascal counterpart of the former C expression, "6 < 7 = 4 < 5", is semantically equivalent to "((6 < 7) = 4) < 5)", which is an invalid Pascal expression. Similarly, C assigns a higher precedence to "<" than to "&&", whereas Pascal assigns a higher precedence to "and" than to "<". Therefore the C code "a < b && c < d", if translated directly into Pascal, would be semantically equivalent to "(a < (b and c)) < d", which is, once again, an illegal Pascal expression. In order to preserve the intended precedence, C expressions must often be parenthesized when translating to Pascal. (See examples 1 and 3 in appendix B).

15. And/or evaluation order. The semantics of the C operator "&&" dictate that if the

first operand evaluates to false then the second operand is not evaluated; i.e. if e1 evaluates to false in the C expression "e1 && e2", e2 will not be evaluated (C reference manual page 181). In Pascal, whether or not the second operand is evaluated is implementation dependent (page 32 of Pascal manual). Similarly, the C semantics of "||" dictate that the second operand is not evaluated if the first operand evaluates to true. In Pascal this is also implementation dependent. Assuming that the Pascal implementation does not correspond to the C standard (and indeed, the Berkeley implementation does not), then one cannot translate the C expression "e1 && e2" to the Pascal expression "e1 and e2" since the evaluation of e2 might produce a side effect. If the "&&" or "||" operator occurs in the expression part of the if-statement, then a straightforward translation is possible: the C statement "if (e1 && e2) ..." can be translated to the Pascal statement "if e1 then if e2 then ...". A more general solution is needed for cases when the "&&" and "||" operators occur in arbitrary expressions. A general solution is indicated by the following example: The C while-stmt

while (e1 && e2) { ... }

can be translated to the Pascal statements

temp1 := e1;
if temp1 then temp2 := e2 else temp2 ::= false;
while (temp1 and temp2) do
begin
...
temp1 := e1;
if temp1 then temp2 :=e2 else temp2 ::= false;
end;

A similar solution exists for the "||" operator. In the current version of the Pascal-to-C and C-to-Pascal translators, it is assumed that the Pascal implementation of "and" and "or" corresponds to the C standard.

16. Control-loop variables. After executing the C for-loop "for (i = 1; i <= 10; i++) {...}", the value of the control variable i is well-defined (it equals 11). However, after executing the Pascal for-loop "for i = 1 to 10 do begin ... end", the value of i is not well-defined (Pascal manual page 39). Therefore it is not safe to translate the above C for loop into the Pascal for loop unless the variable i is not used in the remainder of the

program. There are several solutions to this problem, such as reassigning the final value to the control variable after loop exit. The current version of the C-to-Pascal translator ignores this problem.

As mentioned above, a study of these differences guided the design of ABSIM. For some decisions, such as whether to follow the syntactic conventions of Pascal or C, an arbitrary choice was made. In other cases the GCD was chosen. For instance, as Pascal does not allow expression assignments (point 5) nor initializers (point 12), these are not found in ABSIM. On the other hand, since C does not allow procedures to be local to procedures (point 13) nor arrays with non-zero lower bounds (point 6), ABSIM rules out these constructs as well.

6.3. Source-to-source translators for Pascal and C

This section presents an overview of the Pascal-to-C and C-to-Pascal translators. Defining the canonical form ABSIM, as described in the last section, was the first step in building these translators. The next step was to write two AGs, one translating from C to ABSIM and the other translating from Pascal to ABSIM. By passing these AGs through the INVERT program, the inverse AGs were automatically generated. All four AGs (two originals and two generated by INVERT) were then run through the Linguist [19] AG-based translator-writing-system to produce four translators: Pascal-to-ABSIM, ABSIM-to-Pascal, C-to-ABSIM, and ABSIM-to-C. The composition of appropriate pairs of these are the core Pascal-to-C and C-to-Pascal translators. In addition, each of these translators has some additional software modules. For example, each of the translators has a post-processor, which basically serves as a pretty-printer. The post-processors were generated by the LEX [47] Unix utility. The Pascal-to-C translator also has a preprocessor, discussed in section 6.4, which is responsible for "denesting" nested Pascal procedures and functions. The architecture of the Pascal-to-C translator is presented schematically in figure 6-2. The C-to-Pascal architecture is of a similar nature.

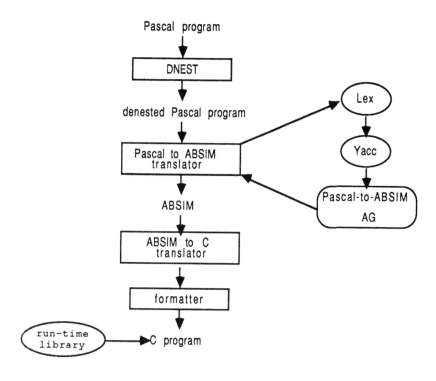

Figure 6-2: Architecture of the Pascal-to-C translator

The following table gives statistics concerning the attribute grammars Pascal-to-ABSIM, C-to-ABSIM, and their inverses, automatically generated by INVERT. It records, for each AG, its length (number of lines), the number of nonterminal symbols, the number of attributes, the number of productions, and the number of semantic rules. It also gives the number of alternating passes required by the AG (using the Linguist system).

AG	#lines	#nonterms	#atts	#prods	#semrule	#pass
Pasc-to-ABSIM	2176	86	252	153	489	4
ABSIM-to-Pasc	2084	91	257	172	524	4
C-to-ABSIM	3004	96	396	173	627	4
ABSIM-to-C	3370	96	378	191	978	5

Figure 6-3: Statistics for the Pascal and C attribute grammars

In translating between programming languages, one often needs to make use of auxiliary routines. For example, complex C I/O operations have no direct counterpart in

Pascal but can be mimicked by Pascal function calls. Similarly, Pascal does not allow for assignments within expressions but C does. To translate a C assignment expression into Pascal, one needs a special Pascal assignment function (see point 5 of section 6.2). These auxiliary functions are written once and put into a library. Each translated program contains an *include* statement, so it can make use of these library routines.

In the current version of the Pascal-to-C and C-to-Pascal translators, comments are stripped from the program before translation. In order to increase the readability and maintainability of the translated program, it is beneficial to retain comments in the translated program. As there may no longer be a one-to-one correspondence between lines in the original and translated programs, some sophistication is needed to do this correctly. See [3] for one suggestion on how this should be done.

The Pascal-to-C and C-to-Pascal translators will not translate any Pascal and C program. They will only translate between a (fairly large) subset of all Pascal and C programs, as indicated in the last section. These translators are limited in their applicability for two reasons. Firstly, manpower considerations dictated that some limitation be placed on the implementation. The language subsets were chosen to be fairly indicative of the different language features in Pascal and C. Once the feasibility of the inversion approach was proven for a certain language feature, other similar language features were not included in the implementation. For example, once Pascal and C arrays were implemented, it was not deemed necessary to implement other aggregate data structures such as Pascal records and C structures, even though there are some differences between the two [28]. For a similar reason the complex I/O commands supported by the C environment were not implemented. This is because the translation of these commands would simply involve the creation of special purpose functions to be included in the Pascal run-time library. Since the main purpose in building these translators was to test out the inversion approach to source-to-source translation, only those language constructs which posed some new difficulty or added a new dimension to the methodology were implemented.

The second reason for implementing language subsets instead of the entire language has already been alluded to: in some instances there is just no good way to translate between different programming language constructs, regardless of the methodology employed. Two examples of this are translating C pointer arithmetic into Pascal and translating Pascal pass by value array parameters into C. (As discussed in the last section and illustrated by example 3 of appendix B, some C pointer arithmetic can be implemented in Pascal in a straightforward manner, and whenever possible the C-to-Pascal translator performs the appropriate translation). Of course, as both languages are Turing equivalent there is theoretically some way of translating any Pascal program into a C program and vice versa[23]. In practice, however, such translations are often useless, as they either take too long to find or are grossly inefficient implementations.

Example translations performed by the Pascal-to-C and C-to-Pascal translators are given in appendix B. In the current implementation of these translators, a program which cannot be translated because it contains non-portable constructs (e.g., complex C pointer arithmetic) either fail to parse or return the translation "ERROR". This gives the user no indication as to where the problem lies and no hints on how to solve the problem. Minimally, a complete system should translate those portions of the program which it can and flag those parts of the program which it cannot. This is the strategy adopted in [10] for translating machine dependent features. Ideally, the system could even suggest possible translations or point out why it is having difficulty with the translation.

---

[23]One possible way to simulate C pointer arithmetic in Pascal is to compute on array indices. For C to simulate Pascal's capability to pass an array by value, a secondary array can be used. This secondary array would be initialized to the value of the original array and then used as the parameter in the function call. Since any change to the secondary array's data would not effect the original array, this would effectively simulate call by value.

6.4. Denesting Pascal procedures and functions

Pascal allows procedures and functions to be declared locally within other procedures and functions. We refer to a Pascal program with a procedure[24] declared locally within another procedure as a *nested* program. In C, nested programs are not allowed. Hence any nested Pascal program must be *denested* when it is translated to C. This entails removing the inner procedure declarations and making them top-level declarations. Furthermore, the run-time environment of these moved procedures must be maintained. The intricacies of this process is illustrated by an example given in figure 6-4.

Let us analyze what happens when procedures B, C, D, and E are denested and made into top level procedures. Since the variables x, y and z are now local to A and inaccessible to the other procedures, we need to provide some mechanism for giving B access to y, C access to x, and D access to z. A naive solution is to make these variables global. A quick analysis reveals that this solution is inadequate, as one needs to maintain multiple copies of these variables upon the run-time stack. An alternative solution, the one implemented in the Pascal-to-C translator, inserts extra pass by reference parameters into the inner procedures. This allows inner procedures to reference variables defined in an outer scope by referencing these new actual parameters. For instance, in the previous example, D would get a new formal parameter, z, and the call to invoke D (in procedure A) would pass z as an actual parameter. In doing this, transitive dependencies need to be taken into consideration. For example, since procedure C needs to reference the variable x and C is invoked from procedure B, B also needs to be able to reference x. And since procedure E invokes procedure B, it too needs to reference x. Using this approach it is possible to denest any Pascal program and produce an equivalent denested one. When applying this method to the program of 6-4, the program of 6-5 is produced. In this example a forward declaration for procedure A needs to be inserted since A is called before it is defined. The following section formally specifies the denesting algorithm.

---

[24] For the remainder of this section, we shall use the term "procedure" to refer to both functions and procedures.

```
program example1(input, output);

    procedure A(x: integer);
    var y, z: integer;

        procedure B;

                procedure C;
                begin
                if x < 10 then A(x);
                write('x = ', x)
                end; {procedure C}

            begin
            C;
            write('y =', y)
            end; {procedure B}

        procedure D;

                procedure E;
                begin
                B
                end; {procedure E}

            begin
            write('z =', z);
            E
            end; {procedure D}

    begin
    y := x;
    z := x;
    x := x + 1;
    D
    end; {procedure A}
begin
A(1)
end. {program example1}
```

Figure 6-4: A nested Pascal program

6.4.1. The denesting algorithm

In this section an algorithm is presented which, given a Pascal program P, will construct a semantically equivalent Pascal program P' such that P' contains no nested procedures. In order to simplify the presentation of this algorithm, a few restrictions are placed on the program P. The end of this section will discuss how these restrictions can

```
program example1(input, output);

procedure A(x: integer); forward;

procedure C(var x: integer);
begin
     if x < 10 then A(x);
     write('x = ', x)
end; {procedure C}

procedure B(var x: integer; var y: integer);
begin
     C(x);
     write('y =', y)
end; {procedure B}

procedure E(var y: integer; var x: integer);
begin
     B(x, y)
end; {procedure E}

procedure D(var y: integer; var x: integer; var z: integer);
begin
     write('z =', z);
     E(y, x)
end; {procedure D}

procedure A;
var y, z: integer;
begin
     y := x;
     z := x;
     x := x + 1;
     D(y, x, z)
end; {procedure A}

begin
     A(1)
end. {program example1}
```

Figure 6-5: The denested Pascal program

be removed. The restrictions are that (i) all variable names in P are unique and (ii) P contains no "forward" declarations[25]. Furthermore, it is assumed that all procedure parameters are either value or variable parameters, not functional or procedural parameters.

---

[25]A forward declaration allows a procedure to be used before it is declared. Forward declarations are used, for instance, when defining mutually recursive procedures.

A variable v is said to be *local to* the procedure A if v is defined in the variable declaration part of A or v is a formal parameter to A. Otherwise v is said to be *nonlocal* to A. A procedure B is said to be *local to* A if B is defined in the procedure declaration part of A. Let P be a Pascal program. The relation UP-OR-LEFT-OF $\subseteq$ (procedures of P $\times$ procedures of P) is defined so that A UP-OR-LEFT-OF B iff (i) B is local to A, or (ii) A and B are local to C and A is defined before (to the left of) B, or (iii) there exists a procedure D such that A UP-OR-LEFT-OF D and D UP-OR-LEFT-OF B.

Given a Pascal program P, the key to denesting P is to determine the extra variables that must be passed to each function in order to maintain the proper run-time environment. For a given procedure A of P, the set of variables that need to be passed as extra parameters is referred to as A's *imports* and denoted *A.imports*. If v $\in$ A.imports, then v must be declared in A's function heading as a new variable parameter (of the appropriate type) and every call to A must include v as a an actual parameter (in the appropriate position of the actual parameter list). Of course, an easy but inefficient solution would be to pass all variables to all procedures. A more elegant solution is to pass the minimal number of variables to each procedure. This notion of *minimality of imports* can be formalized but is not done so here. The computation of the minimal set A.imports entails the computation of the following sets:

1. A.localVars = {v | variable v is local to A}.

2. A.localProcs = {B | procedure B is local to A}.

3. A.upRefs = {v | v is a non-local, non-global variable of A referenced in A's body}. [These nonlocal variables are referenced in A so they certainly need to be to be passed to A once it is denested].

4. A.totalUpRefs = A.upRefs $\cup_{B \in A.localProcs}$ (B.totalUpRefs - A.localVars). [Any procedure B local to A can only be invoked after invoking A. Therefore, if B needs to be passed a variable v, v also has to be accessible to A. If v is local to A then it certainly will be accessible to A. Otherwise it needs to be passed to A].

5. A.upperCalls = {Q | procedure Q is invoked in A's body and (Q UP-OR-LEFT-OF A)}. [If any procedure Q is invoked in A, A needs to have access to the variables imported by Q. If Q's definition is nested in A, then this information has already been recorded in A.totalUpRefs, But if Q's definition is not nested in A, then add Q to the list A.upperCalls].

6. A.totalUpperCalls = A.upperCalls $\cup_{B \in A.localProcs}$ ((B.totalUpperCalls - A.localProcs) - { A }).

7. A.imports = A.totalUpRefs $\cup_{B \in A.totalUpperCalls}$ B.imports. [A needs to import A.totalUpRefs as mentioned previously. Furthermore, let B be a procedure which is invoked from A or from a procedure whose definition is nested in A. Any imports needed by B need to be passed to A, since the invocation of B occurs in A or from a procedure which is invoked after invoking A].

The following chart gives the computation of the sets upRefs, upperCalls, etc., for the procedures of program example1, given in figure 6-4.

procedure	upRefs	totalUpperRefs	upperCalls	totalUpperCalls	Imports
A	$\varnothing$	$\varnothing$	$\varnothing$	$\varnothing$	$\varnothing$
B	{ y }	{ x,y }	$\varnothing$	{ A }	{ x,y }
C	{ x }	{ x }	{ A }	{ A }	{ x }
D	{ z }	{ z }	$\varnothing$	{ B }	{ x,y,z }
E	$\varnothing$	$\varnothing$	{ B }	{ B }	{ x,y }

The computation of A.imports for some procedure A requires the computation of information (including the set of imports) for other procedures of P. An analysis of the algorithm reveals, however, that no circular definitions are entailed. In particular, the sets A.totalUpRefs and A.totalUpperCalls can be computed after the sets B.totalUpRefs and B.totalUpperCalls have been computed for each procedure B local to A. Similarly A.imports can be computed after A.totalUpRefs, A.totalUpperCalls, and B.imports have been computed, for each procedure B such that B UP-OR-LEFT-OF A holds. This is because if B ∈ A.totalUpperCalls then the relation B UP-OR-LEFT-OF A must hold (by definition of A.totalUpperCalls). However, if we relax the restriction mentioned earlier and allow for forward declarations, then the algorithm must be modified so that A.totalUpperCalls also contains any procedure C invoked in A (or in a procedure nested in A), and such that a forward declaration occurs for C before the definition of A. Hence C and A may be mutually recursive and the imports for C and A depend upon one another. In this case the algorithm needs to be modified to compute a least fixed point of the imports required by the mutually recursive procedures.

Loosening the restriction that requires unique names in the program can be done in several ways. The easiest method is to simply make a prepass over the program renaming any duplicate names. This will often result in unnecessary renaming. A better strategy is to rename any computed import if it conflicts with a local variable definition.

Once the list of imports of each procedure is computed, the rest of the denesting algorithm is straightforward. For each procedure A, new formal parameters are constructed corresponding to the set of imports. Every invocation of A is also augmented with these actual parameters (this may call for renaming as described above). Finally, the actual text of the nested procedure needs to be removed from its nested context and placed within the main program. There is a subtle question where the denested procedure should be placed- before or after the procedure it was nested within. Since a procedure B nested in a procedure A can only be invoked from within A's scope, it makes sense to place B before A. Otherwise a forward declaration will be required for B in the denested program. But this strategy cannot guarantee that forward declarations will not be needed. To the contrary, if B contains a call to A, or to any procedure defined outside of A, several forward declarations will be required in the denested program. This is the case of in figure 6-4 where a forward declaration for procedure A is required even though the denested procedures are placed before the procedures they were nested within.

One final point that should be addressed concerns the referencing of components of aggregate data types, such as arrays or records. One could treat a reference to a component of an aggregate as a reference to just that component, or one could treat it as a reference to the entire aggregate. The latter strategy must be adopted in at least some cases when it is impossible to determine which component is being referenced until run-time; e.g., an array reference of the form a[i]. This strategy is probably preferred in all situations, as it will result in passing fewer variable parameters; e.g., instead of passing a[5], a[7], and a[10] as new parameters, only one parameter, a, needs to be passed.

6.4.2. The DNEST pre-processor

The algorithm given above was encoded in a preprocessor to the Pascal-to-C translator. This preprocessor is called DNEST. It was written as an AG and generated by the Linguist AG-based translator writing system. Although the actual algorithm is not that complicated, because a fair amount of information needs to be collected from the program, the generated translator requires a hefty six passes! Part of the reason the translator requires so many passes is due to the alternating pass strategy used by Linguist and the sequential left-to-right information flow required by the algorithm. This is certainly a situation where a more efficient evaluation strategy would significantly improve the performance of the generated translator. (For this reason a new version of the Linguist system incorporates the uniform evaluation strategy [20]).

DNEST is not an invertible translator, although it could have been written as one. There are two features of the translation that are difficult to phrase as RIFs but can be written as generalized RIFs. Firstly, the fact that inner procedures need to be appended before (after) the text of the current procedure means that one trans attribute, as required in RIFs, is not enough. One can easily write this facet of the translation, however, as a GRIF (chapter 5). One trans attribute can be used for text of the current procedure and one trans attribute for the text of nested procedures. A second aspect of the translation which is also difficult to phrase as a pure RIF is the fact that all procedure calls must have additional text appended to them. This text gives the new actual parameters that must be included in the call to the (now denested) procedure. This facet of the translation can be captured using the additive token permuting functions of section 5-2.

The reason why the denesting portion of the translation was not written as part of the main invertible translators is twofold. First of all, since the denesting algorithm requires a fair amount of computation (in terms of attributes and information propagation), it was easier from an engineering point of view to isolate this part of the project into a separate unit and thereby modularize the software development. More important is the fact that inverting this aspect of the translation would have introduced much unwarranted ambiguity into the inverted AG. Given an arbitrary denested Pascal program, it can potentially be "renested" it many different ways. If the denesting algorithm was included in the main invertible translators, any C program with many procedures would be parsable in several different ways, each parse reflecting a unique way to "renest" the procedures. Of course, the ideal translation to produce for this C program is not to "renest" the procedures at all but to produce the isomorphic unnested Pascal program. Therefore the ambiguity that would have been introduced by including the denesting process into the invertible translators is completely unwarranted. Furthermore, even if the inverted translator could have been fine tuned to always choose the parse which left all procedures denested, there still would have been extra unneeded semantics being computed- those semantics that are used in the original AG to denest Pascal programs. In summary, nothing would have been gained by formulating the denesting process as part of the invertible AGs, and much would have been lost in terms of efficiency.

6.5. Summary

In this chapter we have shown how AG inversion can be used in a source-to-source translation system. By using invertible grammars in this context, one is provided with a framework in which to reason about the complexities of bi-directional translators, as well as a tool to perform much of the work. By phrasing the problem as one of finding a canonical form in which to represent all source language programs and writing invertible AGs to and from this canonical form, many of the real difficulties of the translation problem become immediately apparent.

This chapter has also related our experience in using the inversion approach to source-to-source translation in writing translators between C and Pascal. This experiment demonstrated that invertible AGs are a satisfactory tool for describing much of the translators, although the complete system needs to incorporate other modules as well. In conclusion, AG inversion promises to be a useful tool in facilitating source-to-source translations.

Chapter 7

Conclusions and future directions

This thesis has introduced the novel idea of attribute grammar inversion. The main goal of this thesis was to show that given an attribute grammar describing a translation from language L1 to language L2, it is possible to automatically construct the inverse attribute grammar describing the translation from L2 back to L1. The first several chapters described the algorithm to perform this construction and analyzed the properties of inverted AGs.

Part of the reason for studying AG inversion was in order to use the technique to automate the construction of source-to-source translators. Whereas the first part of this thesis concentrated on the theoretical aspects of inversion, the second part of the thesis described how the theory was applied to construct a system for inverting attribute grammars. This system, called INVERT, was then used as a tool to develop bi-directional translators between the Pascal and C programming languages.

Initially the INVERT system accepted only RIF grammars (discussed in chapter 3). Because these AGs are severely limited in practice, it was difficult to use the system to express complex translations. Whereas AGs are extremely powerful and easy to use, RIFs seemed overly restricted and awkward. In particular, attempting to phrase the translations between Pascal and C as RIFs was an arduous chore. For this reason much research was devoted to extending the inversion paradigm to include more powerful constructs. The results of this investigation were given in chapters 4 and 5. Most of these extensions were included in the INVERT system, and the job of writing invertible grammars to translate between Pascal and C became significantly easier.

Future use of the INVERT system may indicate that even further extensions to the system are necessary. Certainly the current implementation can be made more efficient and user friendly. Nonetheless, my experience with INVERT, especially using it to invert the Pascal-to-ABSIM and C-to-ABSIM attribute grammars, surpassed my expectations. I found it quite easy to write no -trivial translations as extended RIFs and am confident that, without too much extra effort, most translations can be written in an invertible manner. By the end of the project it became clear to me that the main issue to be addressed in inverting AGs was not whether translations could be written in an invertible manner, but how to deal with ambiguity in the generated inverse AGs. This latter issue turned out to be far more problematic than I originally imagined. Although my implementation includes some tools to rid ambiguity from the inverse AG, more research into this matter is certainly warranted. This topic will be considered in greater detail in the next section.

Writing an invertible AG requires the writer to think about both translation directions simultaneously. One way to view the work of this thesis is as a methodology for writing two translators at the same time, with tools to check for consistency. In chapter 6 it was demonstrated how invertible AGs can be used to construct source-to-source translators. The methodology centers on the creation of a *greatest common denominator canonical form*, in which to represent all source language programs. This canonical form is a catalogue of the structures common to all the source languages. My experience with this approach was very favorable. The use of a GCD canonical form, coupled with AG inversion, greatly simplified the construction of the Pascal-to-C and C-to-Pascal translators. Nonetheless, using a GCD canonical form does have disadvantages, especially when many source languages are involved. For this reason section 7.2 will discuss alternatives to the GCD approach.

7.1. Many-to-one translations and the ambiguity problem

In section 3.3 it was observed that an inverted AG may be ambiguous even if the original is not ambiguous. Moreover, if the AG G describes a many-to-one translation T, then the inverse AG must be ambiguous. For example, if there exist strings x and y such that $(x,s) \in T$ and $(y,s) \in T$, then the inverted AG G^{-1} will express the one-to-many translation T^{-1} with $(s,x) \in T^{-1}$ and $(s,y) \in T^{-1}$. In such a case the underlying context-free grammar for G^{-1} will contain two parses for s, one translating it to x and the other translating it to y.

The inversion approach to source-to-source translation often results in ambiguous inverse AGs, since the translations from each source language into the canonical form are often many-to-one. For instance, consider a C-to-Pascal translator. Whereas C permits variations on the assignment operator (+=, -=, etc.), Pascal allows only simple assignment (:=). The GCD canonical form would adopt the Pascal convention and allow only simple assignment. Therefore the C strings "X = X + 1", "X += 1", and "X++" would all be translated to the canonical form string "X := X + 1". This would in turn make the inverse translator one-to-many -and ambiguous- since it would specify that "X := X + 1" could be translated to any of the above strings. Another example which produces ambiguity concerns the ordering of declarations. Whereas Pascal requires that all global variable declarations precede procedure and function declarations, the definition of C contains no such requirement. Let F be a function declaration and V a variable declaration. Both C programs "F V" and "V F" would be translated into the canonical form representation "V F", consistent with the Pascal requirement of variable declarations preceding function declarations. This would also introduce ambiguity into the inverse translator.

As mentioned in section 5.3, the ambiguity in the generated inverse AG can create problems for our translators if we rely on a typical deterministic shift/reduce parser. In such a case we have no method for analyzing multiple parses, but arbitrarily choose one parse. If this parse is later invalidated due to as of yet unseen syntax or as of yet uncomputed semantics, we have no method for backtracking. In that section we described two methods incorporated by the INVERT system to help remove ambiguity from the inverse AG. In the generated ABSIM-to-Pascal and ABSIM-to-C AGs I found that the ambiguity problem was not overwhelming. First of all, the amount of ambiguity in the generated inverse grammars was not very significant to begin with. Secondly, the methods incorporated by INVERT, detailed in section 5.3, removed most of the ambiguity. The ambiguity that remained was arbitrarily resolved by the shift/reduce parser without any detrimental effects. It would be helpful to generalize the method of collapsing productions, discussed in section 5.3, so that INVERT could statically detect and remove even more ambiguity from the inverted AG. But even extending this technique will not suffice; if AG inversion is to be a useful tool, a more general mechanism for dealing with the ambiguity problem must be found.

One possible solution to the problem is to add an additional translation layer so that the invertible grammars really do describe one-to-one translations. This approach is illustrated in figure 7-1.

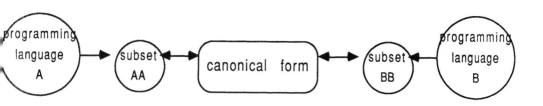

Figure 7-1: A layered approach to source-to-source translation

The basic idea behind this approach is to define subsets of languages A and B (referred to as AA and BB) so that invertible one-to-one AGs from the sublanguages AA and BB into the canonical form can be written. In this scheme, one would first translate a program from language A into a program of AA and then into a program of BB. Since BB is a sublanguage of B, this would also be a program of B. This *layered approach* is very similar to the methodology discussed in [41], except that our approach still makes use of invertible AGs. The language AA should be a "canonical" subset of the language A, meaning that any program in language A should have a representation in language AA (and similarly for languages B and BB). Care must be taken using this approach so that the translators from A to AA and B to BB do not perform more translation than necessary. They should only be responsible for translating concepts that have multiple representations in a language into a unique representation, thereby allowing the translations from AA and BB into the canonical form to be one-to-one. The Pascal-to-C translator described in chapter 5 actually contains one preprocessing stage along these lines. As indicated in section 6.4, the denesting of Pascal procedures is performed in a preprocesser and not in the main invertible translators, precisely because of the ambiguity problem.

This layered approach has some drawbacks. First of all, eliminating all ambiguity also eliminates the possibility of producing optimized translations. For example, consider once again the C-to-Pascal translator. Using the layered approach, the C strings "X = X + 1", "X += 1", and "X++" would all be represented in the canonical sublanguage CC as the string "X = X + 1". This means that the Pascal string "X := X + 1" would always be translated to "X = X + 1", thereby eliminating the possibility of translating it to an optimized version such as "X++". If we simply had an ambiguous grammar which specified that "X := X + 1" had several possible translations, we could choose an optimized translation based upon some metric. This will be discussed further below. Another problem with the layered approach is that it will still not completely guarantee to rid the inverse translator of all ambiguity. As pointed out in section 3.3, even if the original AG is one-to-one, the inverted AG may still be ambiguous!

A more general solution to this problem is the construction of an evaluator for ambiguous AGs. Such a system would allow multiple parses for a given input to be maintained. It would throw away a parse if it (i) determines that the parse is syntactically or semantically invalid, or (ii) determines that a "better" parse exists. Useful metrics for evaluating how "good" a parse is might be based on the length or amount of "structure" of the code generated for the parse; e.g., one might rate the structure of a for-loop higher than the structure of a goto statement and the structure of the C construct "+=" higher than "+".

In order for such a system to work, we need to be able to guarantee that the number of parses for a given input is finite (recall that in AGs, one can have an infinite number of parses using ε-productions, see appendix A). The Epsilon-free RIFs of appendix A are useful for this purpose, since they restrict the use of ε-productions and guarantee a finite number of parses for any given input.

Using these grammars, we could employ Earley's algorithm [16] for finding all parses of the input. Then, using dynamic programming, we could choose the "best" parse from among these. This technique was first formulated for finding the minimum cost correction of an input string to make it a legal sentence of the language in [48]. It was subsequently employed in a Graham-Glanville style code generator [14]. This technique would work fine as long as all syntactically valid parses are also semantically valid. However, when this is not the case, a more sophisticated approach is needed. This is because we cannot eliminate a parse as semantically invalid until attributes are evaluated. But attribute values themselves are dependent upon the parse chosen! Hence we need a strategy for combining syntactic and semantic analysis. A generalized version of *attributed parsing* [53, 50, 34, 62, 63], would be useful in this respect. Using attributed parsing, invalid parses can often be eliminated immediately at parse time. As an example, consider the generated inverse productions of figure 5-5. These productions translate Pascal statements of the form "A := A + B" to C statements of the form "A += B" and statements of the form "A := B" to statements of the form "A = B". Using a standard shift/reduce parser, there will exist a shift/reduce conflict when parsing a string of the form "A := B + C". The parser does not know whether to shift the symbol ':=' (using production $rl1_a$) or to reduce it to the nonterminal assnStmtI (using production $rl1_b$). Using lookahead to determine that $IdI_1.trans \neq IdI_2.trans$ (i.e., 'A' ≠ 'B'), one can immediately rule out production $rl1_a$, thereby resolving the conflict in favor of production rI1$_b$. Note that this requires a generalization of the attributed parsing techniques discussed in the literature so that lookahead can be used to influence parsing.

Much research is still needed to investigate the best approach for an AG evaluation system based on ambiguous grammars. Because ambiguous AGs are useful for a variety of tasks in addition to source-to-source translation (for example, in Graham-Glanville code generation), I believe that such research is valuable in its own right. A start in this direction is given in [66].

7.2. Alternatives to a GCD canonical form

The inversion approach to source-to-source translation, outlined in chapter 6, calls for a construction of a greatest common denominator canonical form. The granularity of this language is such that

- every source language program has a representation in the canonical form,
- every canonical form program that is the image of one translation is expressible as the image of every other translation, and
- the canonical form is not so low level that program structure is thrown away needlessly.

When the number of source languages is small and the languages are closely related to one another then the use of a GCD canonical form is ideal. This was found to be the case in the Pascal-to-C and C-to-Pascal translators where the GCD canonical form ABSIM was used with much success. However, when the number of source languages involved is large and the languages are semantically distant from one another then the use of a GCD canonical form may not be a tenable solution. This is because the GCD canonical form will be reduced to a very low level language. Preserving program structure and producing efficient translators is unlikely. Another fault to this approach is that the addition of another source language to an existing system will require the redesign of the canonical form since the GCD of the languages will change. This can invalidate the existing translators, requiring them to rewritten almost from scratch.

An alternative to the GCD canonical form is a *least common multiple* (LCM) canonical form. This canonical form will contain the high-level constructs found in <u>any</u> source language (in contrast to the GCD canonical form which contained only constructs common to <u>all</u> the source languages). For example, if most source languages contained high-level loop constructs but one language contained only goto statements, the LCM canonical form would contain the high-level loop constructs in addition to goto statements. Using a LCM canonical form, one would write AGs describing the translation <u>from the canonical form to each source language</u> instead of from each source language to the canonical form. The inverse translator would once again be obtained using AG inversion.

The advantage to this approach is that the translators between two similar languages will not be degraded just because some other source language is very different from these two. For example, if two languages have for loops and one does not, the canonical form will still contain for loops. When translating between these two languages for loops will be retained, even though when translating to the third language for loops need to be converted to goto statements. Another advantage to this approach is that adding a new language will cause additions to the canonical form (additional high-level constructs of the new source language) but no deletions. The existing translators can therefore be incrementally updated.

The disadvantages to the LCM approach is that writing the original AGs may become very laborious. Since the canonical form will contain constructs found in all source languages, it can be very big. Writing a translator from this language into each source language can require a substantial amount of work. Furthermore, since many different high-level constructs of the canonical form may map to the same construct in some source language, the inverted AGs may once again be very ambiguous. A thorough investigation into this methodology is warranted.

7.3. AG inversion, source-to-source translators, and software reusability

A major goal of current research in software engineering is to discover ways of reusing software. This goal has so far been very elusive. Unlike hardware technologies, where we have been very successful in building large complex systems from small self-contained modules, we have had relatively little success in incorporating small, autonomous, "prefabricated" software pieces into large scale software projects.

There have been many proposals on how to achieve software reusability. Some of these proposals advocate incremental improvements to existing technologies, such as advanced systems for version control [59]. Other proposals recommend far more radical solutions, such as changing the way we currently program and the adoption of object-oriented methods [36]. It is my belief that there is no one solution to the problem, for there is really not only one problem. Rather, "the" problem of software reusability takes on a plethora of forms depending upon the situation. The problem of reusing software developed on one computer for another computer is quite different than using the same sorting procedure in two different applications.

In this thesis I have addressed one aspect of the software reusability problem which will become an increasingly important consideration in the future. As computer languages and systems continue to proliferate, there will develop an immense demand for programs capable of translating between formats for representing information. Such information may be a program written in a particular programming language or a formatted electronic document. In any case, the problems will be similar: converting information between formats without loosing any of the semantic content. Such conversions are called *source-to-source translations*.

In this thesis I have discussed the *inversion approach to source-to-source translation*. This approach provides a standard methodology and some automated tools for building a system for source-to-source translation. There are two major pillars to the methodology:

the design of a canonical form in which to represent the source languages and the use of attribute grammar inversion to build *bi-directional* translators. The crux of the inversion approach to source-to-source translation is that it puts these two pillars together to build a source-to-source translator. The methodology calls for first identifying a canonical form in which to represent the source languages and then writing invertible AGs from each source language to the canonical form. By automatically inverting the attribute grammars we acquire translators from the canonical form to each source language and by composing the appropriate pair of translators we can translate between any pair of source languages. The inversion approach provides a unified framework for thinking about source-to-source translations. It also provides a powerful tool for creating such translators. Hopefully it will aid in the quest for software reusability.

References

[1] G. Arango, I. Baxter, P. Freeman, C. Pidgeon.
     TMM: Software Maintenance by Transformation.
     IEEE Software 3(3):27-39, 1986.

[2] H. Abramson.
     Definite Clause Translation Grammars.
     In *1984 International Symposium on Logic Programming*, pages 233-241. IEEE,
     1984.

[3] P. F. Albrecht, P. E. Garrison, S. L. Graham. R. H. Hyerle, P. Ip, and
     B. Krieg-Bruckner.
     Source-to-Source Translation: Ada to Pascal and Pascal to Ada.
     SIGPLAN Notices 15(11):183-193, 1980.

[4] Alfred V. Aho, Ravi Sethi, Jeffrey D. Ullman.
     Compilers: Principles, Techniques, and Tools.
     Addison-Wesley, Reading, Massachusetts, 1986.

[5] A. V. Aho and J. D. Ullman.
     Properties of Syntax Directed Translations.
     Journal of Computer and System Sciences 3(3):319-334, August, 1969.

[6] A. V. Aho and J. D. Ullman.
     Syntax Directed Translations and the Pushdown Assembler.
     Journal of Computer and System Sciences 3(1):37-56, February, 1969.

[7] A. V. Aho and J. D. Ullman.
     Translations On A Context Free Grammar.
     Information and Control 19(5):439-475, December, 1971.

[8] Alfred V. Aho and Jeffery D. Ullman.
     The Theory of Parsing, Translation, and Compiling.
     Prentice-Hall, 1972.

[9] Bijan Arbab.
     Compiling Circular Attribute Grammars into Prolog.
     IBM Research and Development 30(3):294-309, May, 1986.

[10] David T. Barnard, David A. Leeson, and Glenn H. Macewen.
     Experience with Translating Euclid to Ada.
     Infor 24(1):59-70, February, 1986.

[11]   Penny Barbe.
       Techniques for Automatic Program Translation.
       In Julius T. Tou (editor), *Software Engineering*, pages 151-165. Academic Press,
           1970.

[12]   G.V. Bochmann.
       Semantic evaluation from left to right.
       Communications of the ACM 19, 1976.
       pp. 55-62.

[13]   James M. Boyle and Monagur N. Muralidharan.
       Program Reusability through Program Transformation.
       IEEE Transactions on Software Engineering SE-10(5):575-588, 1984.

[14]   T. W. Christopher, P. J. Hatcher, and R. Kukuk.
       Using Dynamic Programming to Generate Optimized Code in a Graham-
           Glanville Style Code Generator.
       In *Proceedings of the SIGPLAN '84 Symposium on Compiler Construction*.
           ACM-SIGPLAN, June, 1984.
       Published as Volume 19, Number 6, of *SIGPLAN Notices*.

[15]   Jacques Cohen and Timothy J. Hickey.
       Parsing and Compiling Using Prolog.
       Toplas 9(2):125-163, April, 1987.

[16]   J. Earley.
       An Efficient Context-Free Parsing Algorithm.
       CACM 13(2):94-102, February, 1970.

[17]   Rodney Farrow.
       LINGUIST-86 Yet another translator writing system based on attribute
           grammars.
       In *Proceedings of the SIGPLAN 82 Symposium on Compiler Construction*.
           ACM, June, 1982.

[18]   Rodney Farrow.
       Generating a Production Compiler from an Attribute Grammar.
       IEEE Software 1(4):77-93, October, 1984.

[19]   Rodney Farrow.
       User Manual for Linguist, version 3.0.
       Technical Report, CS Division, EECS Dept., University of California, Berkeley,
           December, 1984.

[20]   Rodney Farrow.
       User Manual for Linguist, version 6.0.
       Technical Report, Declarative Systems, San Jose, California, July, 1986.

[21]   Rodney Farrow and Daniel M. Yellin.
       A Comparison of Storage Optimizations in Automatically-Generated Attribute
           Evaluators.
       Acta Informatica 23(4):393 - 427, July, 1986.

[22] A. R. Feuer and N. H. Gehani.
      A Comparison of the Programming Languages C and Pascal.
      Computing Surveys 14(1), March, 1982.
      pp. 73-92.

[23] Harald Ganzinger and Robert Giegerich.
      Attribute Coupled Grammars.
      In *Proceedings of the SIGPLAN '84 Symposium on Compiler Construction.*
          ACM-SIGPLAN, June, 1984.
      Published as Volume 19, Number 6, of *SIGPLAN Notices*.

[24] H. Ganzinger, R. Giegerich, U. Moncke and R. Wilhelm.
      A Truly Generative Semantics-Directed Compiler Generator.
      In *Proceedings of the SIGPLAN Symposium on compiler construction.* ACM,
          June, 1982.

[25] Robert Giegerich.
      *On the Relation between Descriptional Composition and Evaluation of Attribute
          Coupled Grammars.*
      Technical Report, University of Dortmund, D-4600 Dortmund 50, West
          Germany, February, 1986.
      Preliminary version.

[26] David Gries.
      The Science of Programming.
      Springer-Verlag, Berlin-Heidelberg-New York, 1981.

[27] S. P. Harbison and G. L. Steele Jr.
      C: A Reference Manual.
      Prentice-Hall, Inc., Englewood Cliffs, N. J., 1984.

[28] Vincent Hayward.
      Compared Anatomy of the Programming Languages Pascal and C.
      SIGPLAN Notices 21(5), May, 1986.
      pp. 50-60.

[29] E. Irons.
      A Syntax Directed Compiler for ALGOL-60.
      CACM 4:51-55, 1961.

[30] M. Jazayeri, W.F. Ogden, and W.C. Rounds.
      The intrinsically exponential complexity of the circularity problem for attribute
          grammars.
      Communications of the ACM 18, 1975.

[31] M. Jazayeri and K.G. Walter.
      Alternating semantic evaluator.
      In *Proceedings of ACM 1975 Annual Conference*, pages 230-234. ACM, 1975.

[32] K. Jensen and N. Wirth.
      Pascal User Manual and Report, Third Edition.
      Springer-Verlag, Berlin-Heidelberg-New York, 1985.
      Revised by A. Mickel and J. Miner.

[33]   S.C. Johnson.
        Yacc: Yet Another Compiler-compiler.
        Technical Report 32, Bell Laboratories, Murray Hill, N.J., 1975.

[34]   Neil D. Jones and C. Michael Madsen.
        Attribute-Influenced LR Parsing.
        In G. Goos and J. Hartmanis (editor), *Lecture Notes in Computer Science 94*,
            pages 393-407. Springer-Verlag, Berlin-Heidelberg-New York, 1980.

[35]   W. N. Joy, S. L. Graham, C. B. Haley, M. K. McKusick, and P. B. Kessler.
        Berkeley Pascal User's Manual, Version 3.0 - July 1983.
        Technical Report, Department of Electrical Engineering and Computer Science,
            University of California, Berkeley, July, 1983.

[36]   G. E. Kaiser and D. Garlan.
        Composing Software Systems from Reusable Building Blocks.
        Technical Report, Department of Computer Science, Columbia University, July,
            1986.

[37]   U. Kastens.
        Ordered attribute grammars.
        Acta Informatica 13:229-256, 1980.

[38]   Uwe Kastens, Brigitte Hutt, and Erich Zimmermann.
        GAG:A Practical Compiler Generator.
        In *Lecture Notes in Computer Science 141*. Spring-Verlag, Berlin-Heidelberg-
            New York, 1982.

[39]   Takuya Katayama.
        Translation of Attribute Grammars into Procedures.
        ACM TOPLAS 6(3):345-369, July, 1984.

[40]   Boris Katz and Patrick H. Winston.
        A Two-Way Language Interface.
        In P. Degano and E. Sandewall (editor), *Integrated Interactive Computing
            Systems.* North-Holland, , 1983.

[41]   Bernd Krieg-Bruckner.
        Language Comparison and Source-To-Source Translation.
        In P. Pepper (editor), *Program Transformation and Programming Environments*,
            pages 299 - 304. Springer-Verlag, 1984.

[42]   K. Kennedy and S. K. Warren.
        Automatic generation of efficient evaluators for attribute grammars.
        In *Conference Record of the Third ACM symposium on Principles of
            Programming Languages.* ACM, 1976.

[43]   D. E. Knuth.
        Semantics of context-free languages.
        Mathematical Systems Theory 2:127-145, 1968.
        correction in volume 5, number 1.

[44]   Richard E. Korf.
         Change of Representation by Program Transformation.
         Technical Report, Department of Computer Science, Carnegie-Mellon
            University, December, 1980.
         Thesis proposal.

[45]   K. Koskimies, K-J. Raiha, and M. Sarjakoski.
         Compiler Construction Using Attribute Grammars.
         In *Proceedings of the SIGPLAN Symposium on compiler construction.* ACM,
            June, 1982.

[46]   R. Krishnaswamy and A. Pyster.
         On the Correctness of Semantic-Syntax-Directed Translations.
         Journal of the ACM 27(2):338-355, 1980.

[47]   M. E. Lesk.
         Lex - A Lexical Analyzer Generator.
         Technical Report 39, Bell Laboratories, Murray Hill, N.J., October, 1975.

[48]   G. Lyon.
         Syntax-Directed Least-Errors Analysis for Context Free Languages: A Practical
            Approach.
         Communications of the ACM 17(1):3-14, January, 1974.

[49]   S. Mamrak, M. Kaelbling, C. Nicholas, and M. Share.
         A Software System To Support The Exchange Of Electronic Manuscripts.
         Communications of the ACM 30(5):408-414, May, 1987.

[50]   D. Milton and C. Fischer.
         LL(k) parsing for attributed grammars.
         In H. A. Maurer (editor), *Lecture Notes in Computer Science 7*, pages 422 - 430.
            Springer-Verlag, Berlin-Heidelberg-New York, 1979.

[51]   Kari-Jouko Raiha, M. Saarinen, E. Soisalon-Soininen and M. Tienari.
         The Compiler Writing System HLP (Helsinki Language Processor).
         Technical Report A-1978-2, Dept. of Computer Science, Univ. of Helsinki, 1978.

[52]   Steven P. Reiss.
         Inverse Translation: The Theory of Practical Automatic Programming.
         PhD thesis, Yale University, December, 1977.

[53]   B. Rowland.
         Combining parsing and evaluation for attributed grammars.
         Technical Report 308, University of Wisconsin-Madison, 1977.

[54]   Yoav Shoham and Drew V. McDermott.
         Knowledge Inversion.
         In *Proceedings of the 4th National Conference of AI*, pages 295 - 299. American
            Association for AI, Austin, Texas, August, 1984.

[55]   Sharon Sickel.
         Invertibilty of Logic Programs.
         In *Proceedings of the Fourth Wokshop on Automatic Deduction*, pages 103-109.
            , February, 1979.

[56] Michael Sonnenschein.
      Global Storage Cells for Attributes in an Attribute Grammar.
      Acta Informatica 22():397 - 420, , 1985.

[57] T. B. Steele, Jr.
      UNCOL: The Myth and the Fact.
      Annual Review in Automatic Programming.
      Pergamon Press, 1961.
      pp. 325-344.

[58] Stan Szpakowicz.
      Logic Grammars.
      Byte 12(9):185-195, August, 1987.

[59] W. F. Tichy.
      RCS- A System for Version Control.
      SoftwarePractice&Experience 15(7):637-654, July, 1985.

[60] S. K. Warren.
      The coroutine model of attribute grammar evaluation.
      PhD thesis, Rice University, May, 1976.

[61] David H. D. Warren.
      Logic Programming and Compiling Writing.
      Software Practice and Experience 10:97-125, 1980.

[62] David A. Watt.
      Rule splitting and attribute-directed parsing.
      In G. Goos and J. Hartmanis (editor), *Lecture Notes in Computer Science 94*,
          pages 363 - 392. Springer-Verlag, Berlin-Heidelberg-New York, 1980.

[63] Reinhard Wilhelm.
      Inverse Currying Transformations on Attribute Grammars.
      In *Conference Record of the Eleventh ACM Symposium on Principles of
          Programming Languages*, pages 140-147. ACM, January, 1984.

[64] Daniel M. Yellin.
      A Survey of Tree-Walk Evaluation Strategies for Attribute Grammars.
      Technical Report, Department of Computer Science, Columbia University, New
          York, New York 10027, September, 1984.

[65] Daniel M. Yellin.
      User manual for the Invert system, Version 1.0.
      Technical Report, Department of Computer Science, Columbia University, New
          York, New York 10027, January, 1987.

[66] Daniel M. Yellin.
      Generalized Attributed Parsing.
      Technical Report, IBM, October, 1987.

[67] Daniel M. Yellin and Eva-Maria M. Mueckstein.
      The Automatic Inversion of Attribute Grammars.
      IEEE Transactions on Software Engineering SE-12(5):590 - 599, May, 1986.

[68]   Chae Woo Yoo.
        An Approach to the Transportation of Computer Software.
        Information Processing Letters 21:153-157, 1985.

Appendix A

AGs using ERROR and computability

Traditionally, AGs have been based on underlying context-free grammars which are unambiguous. In this way any AG G defines a <u>function</u> T. Any string w in the domain of the context-free grammar is considered to be in the domain of the translation T. Since the context-free grammar is unambiguous, T(w) is unambiguously defined. For our purposes, however, it is convenient to view an AG as specifying a <u>relation</u> R. We therefore allow the underlying context-free grammar to be ambiguous. If a string w has two parse trees associated with it, one translating w to x and the other to x′, then both (w,x) and (w, x′) are in the relation R. Furthermore, we do not require that the domain of R be context-free. As described in section 2.1.1.2, we augment the AG with the special symbol ERROR. If a parse for w produces the translation ERROR then that parse is *invalid*. A string w is in the domain of R if and only if there exist some parse for w producing a non-ERROR translation.

In this appendix we show that using this definition, it is not decidable for an arbitrary AG G and input w, whether or not there is a valid parse tree for w. Of course, this is certainly the case if any individual semantic function of the AG is not a totally recursive function. But in the following theorem, we assume that all the semantic functions of the AG are totally recursive.

Theorem 1: For an arbitrary AG G (using ERROR) and string w, it is undecidable whether or not w is in the domain of the translation defined by G

Proof: We will prove this theorem by reducing a version of the well-known halting problem to our problem. Let $T(w,n) = 1$ if n is an integer and the nth Turing machine halts on input w and 0 otherwise. The boolean function $G(y, k)$ returns the value true if y is of the form w#n, k is an integer, and the nth Turing machine halts on input w in less than or equal to k steps. Otherwise G returns the value false. Clearly G is a total recursive function. Consider the AG of figure A-1. The productions for the nonterminal 'string' (deriving arbitrary strings over some alphabet) and for 'integer' (deriving integers) are not shown.

S ::= A E.
    S.trans = if not(E.accept) then ERROR
        else Concat(A.trans, E.trans);
    E.num_in = 1;
    E.input_string = A.trans;

A ::= string # integer.
    A.trans = Concatenate(string.trans, '#', integer.trans);

E0 ::= E1 E2.
    E0.trans = Concat(E1.trans, E2.trans);
    E0.num_out = E2.num_out;
    E0.accept = E1.accept or E2.accept;
    E1.num_in = E0.num_in;
    E1.input_string = E0.input_string;
    E2.num_in = E1.num_out;
    E2.input_string = E0.input_string;

E ::= .
    E.trans = "1";
    E.num_out = E.num_in + 1;
    E.accept = G(input_string,E.num_in);

Figure A-1: A non-computable AG

The underlying context-free grammar of this AG derives strings of the form w#n. The AG specifies the translation $\{(w\#n, w\#n1^k)| G(w\#n,k) = 1\}$ and makes use of only totally recursive semantic functions. Nonetheless, it is easy to see that there is a non-ERROR parse tree for input w#n iff there exists a $k > 0$, such that the nth Turing machine accepts w in less than or equal to k steps. Hence determining whether or not there is a non-ERROR parse for a given input is equivalent to computing $T(w,n)$ which is not decidable. **End of proof.**

Although this theorem is interesting theoretically, it does not represent a serious impediment for using AGs (with ERROR) in practice. This is because if we restrict our attention to AGs in which there is at most a finite number of parses for any string w, then it is decidable whether or not w is in the domain of translation. We will now define a subset of RIFs which can be shown to be computable.

Recall that in section 2.2 it was shown that RIFs are equivalent to AGs. It was stated at that time that by eliminating ε-productions from RIFs, they lose some of their computational power. *Epsilon Free RIF Grammars (EF-RIFs)* are defined to be those RIFs whose underlying context-free grammar has a form similar to *Chomsky Normal Form* (see [8] for instance). Formally, an EF-RIF is a RIF obeying the following restraints:

1. If any production has ε on the right hand side, then the production is [p: S ::= ε] (S is the goal symbol).

2. The goal symbol S does not appear on the right hand side of any production.

3. Any production with nonterminals on the right hand side has at least two nonterminals or a nonterminal and terminals on the right hand side.

4. If a production contains only one nonterminal X on the right hand side, all the token permuting functions in the token permuting clause computing the distinguished attribute are of the form Concatenate(α_1, X.trans, α_2), where $\alpha_1 \alpha_2 \neq \varepsilon$.

5. If any production [p: X ::= α], where α is a terminal string, has the distinguished semantic function X.trans = ε, then X = S.

The first two restraints limit the number of ε productions in the grammar. The third restraint prevents "looping"; i.e., it prevents derivations of the form $X \overset{*}{\Rightarrow} X$ and therefore prevents associating an infinite number of semantic trees to any given input. The fourth and fifth restraints guarantee that EF-RIFs are <u>closed under the inversion algorithm</u>. Running an EF-RIF through the inversion algorithm of chapter 3 will produce an EF-RIF.

EF-RIFs are interesting for two reasons. First of all, unlike AGs (using ERROR), or even RIFs, EF-RIFs can be shown to be computable. That is, given an EF-RIF and any string, there is a bounded amount of work that needs to be done to determine whether or not the string is in the domain of the translation described by the EF-RIF. The proof of this result is left as an exercise for the reader. The second reason RIFs are interesting is because the translations they define are properly included in the class of translations defined by RIFs, as illustrated by the following theorem:

Theorem 2: If T is translation described by an EF-RIF then there is a constant c such that for all (w,x) in T, w $\neq \varepsilon$, $|x| \leq c|w|$.

Proof: This proof makes use of the following definition: The *length* of token permuting function $f(Y_1,...,Y_n) = \text{Concatenate}(\beta_0, Y_{i_1}, \beta_1, Y_{i_2},..., Y_{i_n}, \beta_n)$, denoted *length(f)*, is equal to $|\beta_0 \beta_1 ... \beta_n|$.

Let T be a translation described by an EF-RIF G. We can find a constant k such that for any production [p: $X_0 ::= \alpha_0 X_1 \alpha_1 X_2 ... X_{n_p} \alpha_{n_p}$], each token permuting function of the token permuting clause defining X_0.trans has length $\leq k$. Let $w \neq \varepsilon$, (w,x) in T, and ST be a semantic tree in G translating w to x. Since the right hand side of any production in ST contains either a terminal or at least two nonterminals, the number of productions in ST is $\leq 2|w| - 1$. Hence $|x| \leq k(2|w| - 1)$. The theorem is shown to be true by letting c = 2k. **End of proof.**

This theorem states that EF-RIFs are less powerful than regular RIFs. Compare this theorem with the following lemma concerning syntax-directed translation schema given in [5].

Lemma 3: If T is a syntax directed translation then there is a constant c such that for all $w \neq \varepsilon$ in the domain of T there is an x such that (w,x) is in T and $|x| \leq c|w|$.

Theorem 2 is even stronger than lemma 3; for syntax-directed translation schema all we can insure is that if w is in the domain of the translation, then there is some x such that (w,x) is in T and that $|x| \leq c|w|$. But for EF-RIFs we can insure that for all (w,x) in T this property holds. Does this mean that syntax-directed translation schema are more powerful than EF-RIFs? The following theorem clarifies this point.

Theorem 4: There are translations expressible by syntax-directed translation schema that are not expressible by EF-RIFs and vice versa.

Proof: The translation ($'a^i b^j c^k'$, $'OK \ a^i b^j c^k'$) when $i = j = k$ and ($'a^i b^j c^k'$, $'Not \ OK$ $a^i b^j c^k'$) otherwise is not a syntax directed translation (since the range is not context-free) but can be expressed as a EF-RIF (see figure 2-4). Hence there are translations expressible by EF-RIFs but not expressible by a syntax-directed translation schema.

On the other hand, there are translations that can be expressed by syntax-directed translation schema and not by RIFs. For example, (a^i, a^j), $j \geq i$, cannot be expressed by an EF-RIF (theorem 2), but can be expressed by a syntax-directed translation scheme. **End of proof.**

The only reason that syntax-directed translation schema can perform translations not expressible by EF-RIFs is due to the fact that EF-RIFs do not allow ε-productions. Should we require syntax-directed translation schema to obey a normal form similar to EF-RIFs, then syntax-directed translation schema would be properly contained in the translations performed by EF-RIFs.

Appendix B

Pascal-to-C and C-to-Pascal translations

This appendix presents several examples of translations performed by the Pascal-to-C and C-to-Pascal translators. Each example contains a Pascal and C program. The first one given is the original program. It is followed by the translated program. Most programs are taken from the reference manuals or from text books.

Example 1
```
int dType(c) int c; {
    if (c >= 'a' && c <='z' || c >= 'A' && c <= 'Z')
        return('a');
    else if (c >= '0' && c <= '9')
        return('0');
    else { printf("%s%d", "Function dType returning the value", c);
        return(c);
    }
}
```

```
#include "pasLib.i"
function dType(c: integer): integer;
label 1;
begin
    if ((c >= ord('a')) and (c <= ord('z'))) or
       ((c >= ord('A')) and (c <= ord('Z')))
    then begin dType := ord(('a'));
        goto 1
        end
    else if (c >= ord('0')) and (c <= ord('9'))
        then begin dType := ord(('0'));
            goto 1
            end
        else begin
            write('Function dType returning the value', c);
                begin dType := (c);
                goto 1
                end
            end;
    1: end;
```

Example 2
```
typedef int intArray[10];
void bubbleSort(S)
intArray S;
{
    int beginIndex = 0, endIndex = 9, i;

    for (i = beginIndex; i <= endIndex - 1; i++)
        {
          int j;
          for (j = endIndex; j >= i + 1; j--)
              {
              if (S[j] < S[j-1] )
                  {
                  char temp = S[j-1];
                  S[j-1] = S[j];
                  S[j] = temp;
                  }
              }
        }
}
```

```
#include  "pasLib.i"
type intArray = array [0 .. 9] of integer;

procedure bubbleSort(var S: intArray);
label  1;

var beginIndex, endIndex, i: integer;
   j: integer;
   temp: char;

begin
    beginIndex := 0;
    endIndex := 9;
    for i := beginIndex to endIndex - 1 do
    begin
        for j := endIndex downto i + 1 do
        begin
            if S [j] < S [j - 1]
            then begin
                temp := chr ( S[j - 1]);
                S[j - 1] := S[j];
                S[j] := ord(temp)
            end
        end
    end;
1: end;
```

Example 3
```
int dayTable[2][13];

void monthDay(year, yearday, pmonth, pday)
int year, yearday; int *pmonth, *pday;
{
    int i, leap;

    leap = year/4 == 0 && year/100 != 0 || year/400 == 0;
    for  (i = 1; yearday > dayTable[leap][i]; i++)
        yearday -= dayTable[leap][i];
    *pmonth = i;
    *pday = yearday;
}
```

```
#include  "pasLib.i"

var dayTable: array[0..1,0..12] of integer;

procedure monthDay(year, yearday: integer; var pmonth, pday: integer);
label  1;
var i, leap: integer;

begin
    leap := boolToInt(((year/4= 0) and (year/100<>0)) or (year/400=0));
    i := 1;
    while yearday > dayTable[leap, i] do
    begin
        yearday := yearday - dayTable[leap, i];
        postfixINC(i)
    end;
    pmonth := i;
    pday := yearday;
1: end;
```

Example 4

```c
typedef int numbers[20];

void shellsort(v, n)
numbers v; int n;
{
int i, j, gap = 1, temp;

do gap = 3 * gap + 1; while (gap <= n);
for (gap /= 3; gap > 0; gap /= 3)
  for (i = gap; i <= n - 1; i++) {
    temp = v[i];
    for (j = i - gap; (j >= 0) && (v[j] > temp); j -= gap)
      v[j + gap] = v[j];
    v[j] = temp;
  }
}
```

```pascal
#include  "pasLib.i"
type numbers = array [0..19] of integer;
procedure shellsort(var v: numbers; n: integer);
label  1;
var i, j, gap, temp: integer;

begin
     gap := 1;
     repeat gap := 3 * gap + 1
     until not ( gap <= n );
     gap := gap / 3;
     while gap > 0 do
     begin
          for i := gap to n - 1 do
          begin
               temp := v[i];
               j := i - gap;
               while (j >= 0) and (v[j] > temp) do
               begin
                    v[j + gap] := v[j];
                    j := j - gap
               end;
               v[j] := temp
          end;
     gap := gap / 3
     end;
1: end;
```

Example 5
```
program main(input, output);
var a, b: integer;

procedure badSwap( x, y :integer);   var temp: integer;
begin   temp := x;  x := y;
     y := temp
end;

procedure goodSwap(var x, y :integer); var temp: integer;
begin   temp := x;  x := y;
     y := temp
end;

procedure badAndGoodSwap(var s, t: integer);
begin badSwap(s,t); goodSwap(s,t)
end;

begin
write('input two variables'); read(a, b);
badAndGoodSwap(a, b); write('a =', a, 'b =', b)
end.
```

```
#include <stdio.h>
#include "cLib.h"

void  badSwap( x, y) int x, y; {
     int  temp;  temp = x;
     x = y;  y = temp;
     }

void  goodSwap(x, y) int *x, *y;{
     int  temp;  temp = *x;
     *x = *y;  *y = temp;
     }

void  badAndGoodSwap(s, t) int *s, *t;{
     badSwap(*s, *t); goodSwap(s, t);
     }

int a, b;
main ( ){
     printf ("%s", "input two variables"); scanf("%d%d", &a, &b);
     badAndGoodSwap(&a, &b); printf("%s%d%s%d", "a =", a, "b =", b);
     }
```

Example 6
```
program main(input, output);
  const lowerBounds = 10;
     upperBounds = 20;

  type intArray = array [10 .. 20] of integer;

  var invoice: intArray;
     num, i: integer;

function total(var list: intArray; n:integer): integer;
  var i, sum: integer;
  begin
     total := 0;
     if n <= upperBounds - lowerBounds
     then begin
          sum := 0;
          for i := lowerBounds to upperBounds do
               begin
               sum := sum + list[i];
               total := sum
               end
          end
  end;

begin
     write('enter number of integers  ');
     read(num);
     write('enter integers  ');
     for i := 0 to num - 1 do
          read(invoice[i + lowerBounds]);
     write('sum =', total(invoice, num))
end.
```

Example 6 continued

```c
#include  <stdio.h>
#include  "cLib.h"

#define  lowerBounds  10
#define  upperBounds  20

typedef int intArray[11];

int total(list, n) intArray list; int n;
{
    int i, sum;
    int tempFuncVal;
    tempFuncVal = 0;
    if (n <= upperBounds - lowerBounds)
    {
        sum = 0;
        for (i = lowerBounds; i <= upperBounds; i++)
        {
            sum = sum + list[i - 10];
            tempFuncVal =  sum;
            }
        }
    return tempFuncVal;
    }

int num, i;
intArray invoice;

main ( )
{
printf("%s", "enter number of integers");
scanf("%d", &num);
printf("%s", "enter integers");
for(i = 0; i <= num - 1; i++)
    scanf("%d", &invoice[i + lowerBounds - 10]);
 printf("%s%d", "sum =", total(invoice, num));
 }
```

Example 7
```
type arrayData = array [1 .. 10] of integer;

procedure insertsort(var A: arrayData;  var B: arrayData);
var numberInserted, max: integer;
   i: integer;

   procedure insert(item: integer; var number: integer; var C: arrayData);
   var itemIndex: integer;
      index: integer;

      function itemLocation(dat: integer; num: integer; var D: arrayData): integer;
      var first, last: integer;
         middle: integer;

      begin
         if dat > D[num]
         then itemLocation := num + 1
         else begin
            first := 1;
            last := num;
            repeat
                middle := (first + last) div 2;
                if dat < D[middle]
                then last := middle - 1
                else first := middle + 1;
            until (dat = D[middle]) or (last < first);
            if (dat <= D[middle]) then itemLocation := middle
            else itemLocation := middle + 1
            end
      end;

   begin
      itemIndex := itemLocation(item, number, C);
      for index := number downto itemIndex
          do C[index + 1] := C[index];
      C[itemIndex] := item;
      number := number + 1
   end;

begin
   max := 10;
   numberInserted := 1;
   B[1] := A[1];
   for i := 2 to max
      do insert(A[i], numberInserted, B)
end;
```

Example 7 continued
```
#include  <stdio.h>
#include  "cLib.h"

typedef int arrayData[10];

int itemLocation(dat, num, D) int dat; int num; arrayData D;
{
     int  first, last;
     int  middle;
     int  tempFuncVal ;
     if (dat >  D[num -  1]) tempFuncVal = num + 1;
     else {
          first =  1;
          last =  num;
          do {
               middle =  intDivides ((first + last),  2);
               if (dat < D[middle -  1]) last = middle - 1;
               else  first =  middle + 1;;
          } while (!((dat == D[middle -  1]) || (last < first)));
          if ((dat <= D[middle -  1])) tempFuncVal =  middle;
          else tempFuncVal = middle + 1;
     }
     return tempFuncVal;
}

void  insert(item, number, C) int item; int *number; arrayData C;
{
     int  itemIndex;
     int  index;
     itemIndex = itemLocation(item, *number, C);
     for (index = *number; index >= itemIndex; --index)
          C[index + 1 - 1] =  C[index - 1];
     C[itemIndex - 1] = item;
     *number = *number + 1;
}

void  insertsort(A,  B) arrayData A; arrayData B;
{
     int numberInserted, max;
     int i;
     max =  10;
     numberInserted =  1;
     B[1 -  1] =  A[1 - 1];
     for(i =  2; i <=  max; i ++) insert(A[i - 1], &numberInserted,  B);
}
```

Example 8
```
procedure X(a: integer);

var numYcalls, numZcalls, numBcalls, i :integer;

    function Y(d: integer): integer;

        function Z(g, h: integer): integer;
        begin
        numZcalls := numZcalls + 1;
        if numZcalls < 10 then Z := Y(g + h) else Z := g + h
        end;

    begin
    numYcalls := numYcalls + 1;
    if d < 10 then Y := Z(d + 1, d + 1) else Y:= 100
    end;

    function A: integer;
        function B: integer;
        begin
        numBcalls := numBcalls + 1;
        B := Y(a)
        end;
    begin
    A := B
    end;
begin
numYcalls := 0;
numZcalls := 0;
numBcalls := 0;
i := A;
write('numYcalls=', numYcalls, 'numZcalls=', numZcalls, 'numBcalls=',
    numBcalls, 'i=', i)
end;
```

Example 8 continued

```
#include  <stdio.h>
#include  "cLib.h"

int  Z(g, h, numYcalls, numZcalls) int g, h; int *numYcalls; int *numZcalls;
{
     int tempFuncVal;
     *numZcalls = *numZcalls + 1;
     if (*numZcalls < 10) tempFuncVal = Y(g + h, numZcalls, numYcalls);
     else tempFuncVal = g + h;
     return tempFuncVal;
     }

int Y(d, numZcalls, numYcalls) int d; int *numZcalls; int *numYcalls;
{
     int tempFuncVal;
     *numYcalls = *numYcalls + 1;
     if (d < 10) tempFuncVal = Z(d + 1, d + 1, numYcalls, numZcalls);
     else tempFuncVal = 100;
     return tempFuncVal;
     }

int B(numYcalls, numZcalls, numBcalls, a)
     int *numYcalls; int *numZcalls; int *numBcalls; int *a;
{
     int tempFuncVal;
     *numBcalls = *numBcalls + 1;
     tempFuncVal = Y(*a, numZcalls, numYcalls);
     return tempFuncVal;
     }
int A(numYcalls, numZcalls, a, numBcalls) int *numYcalls; int *numZcalls;
                         int *a; int *numBcalls;
{    int tempFuncVal;
     tempFuncVal = B(numYcalls, numZcalls, numBcalls, a);
     return tempFuncVal;
     }

void X(a) int a;
{
     int numYcalls, numZcalls, numBcalls, i;
     numYcalls = 0;
     numZcalls = 0;
     numBcalls = 0;
     i = A(&numYcalls, &numZcalls, &a, &numBcalls);
     printf("%s%d%s%d%s%d%s%d", "numYcalls=", numYcalls,"numZcalls=",
                numZcalls, "numBcalls=", numBcalls, "i=", i);
     }
```